# Value Investing Essentials

## Principles, Strategies, and Insights

ABHISHEK PARIHAR

ISBN: 9798882651373

# REQUEST TO REVIEW

Dear Reader,

Thank you for embarking on this journey with me. Before you delve into the pages ahead, I would like to extend a humble request. Your feedback is invaluable to me. As you navigate through the principles, strategies, and insights shared within these pages, I encourage you to keep a keen eye and an open mind.

Your thoughts, critiques, and suggestions will not only help me refine and improve future editions but will also contribute to the collective knowledge of our community of investors. Whether you find resonance in the concepts presented or encounter areas for improvement, I eagerly await your insights.

Please consider sparing a moment to share your thoughts, whether through a review, a message, or simply in conversation. Your contribution will shape the trajectory of this work and, hopefully, aid fellow readers on their journey towards financial empowerment.

Thank you for your time, your engagement, and your commitment to learning.

Warm regards,

Abhishek Parihar

# FOREWORD

Dear Reader,

It gives me immense pleasure to present this comprehensive guidebook on stock market analysis and wealth creation for novice investors and traders.

Having been an active market participant and observer for over two decades, I have been privileged to benefit from the wisdom of numerous mentors, authors, practitioners, academics and philosophers of the financial markets. Distilling my learnings and experiences through this book is an endeavour to pay forward the same guidance I gained early on to aspiring students of the market today.

Across chapters, we traverse through not just technical concepts but also the timeless mental models, risk management tenets, behavioural techniques, and empirical lessons that are essential to build trading expertise. Beyond mechanical strategies, imbibing the foundational thinking skills is vital to stand the test of ever-changing financial landscapes.

This book marks the starting point of a structured curriculum for beginners to elevate their market hypothesis development, analytical modelling, statistical back testing and quantification capabilities. A learning journey that begins here with the right building blocks can culminate in mastery over the arcs of market cycles.

My sincere appreciation to all my mentors, peers, professors and students who have shaped my perspectives over lifelong learning. Specifically, I thank my wife and daughters for their steadfast support behind this initiative. I hope you find the book valuable in your own market education. Keep compounding your knowledge.

With warmth and Yours in Learning,

Abhishek Parihar

"SUCCESSFUL INVESTING IS NOT ABOUT PREDICTING THE FUTURE, BUT UNDERSTANDING THE PRESENT AND MAKING INFORMED DECISIONS."

# OPENING NOTE FROM AUTHOR

This book will not instantly make you a profitable trader. Consider it the first stepping stone that provides a structured curriculum covering core foundations across trading styles, markets and techniques.

Internalize the concepts, rigorously track learnings and progress to the next book in the series. In a systematic fashion over 3 books and 3 months, we will progress from beginner to experienced trader and investor.

# WARNING NOTE FROM AUTHOR

- **<u>Never initiate real money trades without stop loss orders in place</u>**.

- Avoid reckless trading without appropriate risk management.

- Do not trade purely based on tips or recommendations without understanding reasons.

- Follow a strict learning plan and trading journal to incrementally build your own skills.

- There are no shortcuts to developing trading expertise.

# HOW TO READ THIS BOOK

Dear Reader,

I'm excited for you to embark on this comprehensive guide to stock market analysis and wealth creation. Here are some tips to maximize your learning from this book:

- **Read Slowly and Take Notes**

Don't rush through the dense concepts. Read attentively and take handwritten notes on key principles, techniques and examples. Summarize core lessons from each chapter in your own words. This will accelerate retention and connect examples to real life charts you'll subsequently analyse.

- **Learn-By-Doing**

True mastery will come only from implementing the strategies yourself. After finishing each chapter, dig into historical charts to identify similar patterns and test techniques yourself. Replay past market scenarios and predict how you would have traded based on signals covered.

- **Use Multiple Resources**

Supplement learnings with online videos, courses and books. Watch how experts analyse charts and apply concepts in real-time. A multifaceted approach across resources develops a robust understanding.

- **Maintain Trading Journal**

Keep a diary noting ah-ha concepts, new techniques learned, questions raised and tracking your accuracy in identifying past chart patterns. This accelerates the learning curve through active recall.

Now let's look at sources for historical charts:
- Leading financial portals like Money control, Yahoo Finance - Offer interactive charts with indicator overlays and analysis tools for Indian stocks and indices. Easy to register and access data up to 10 years back.
- Broker platforms like Zerodha Kite, Upstox - Provide charting capabilities with indicators and drawing tools for back testing purpose within their trading platforms and apps. Sign up for free paper trading account.
- Tradingview - Provides advanced interactive charting platform and social community. Availability of scripts and algos to back test strategies systematically. Offers global exchange data.
- NSE India site - Official source for end of day prices, volumes and historical index values downloadable in easy csv format up to 10 years.
- Investing.com - Provides reliable historical daily and intraday charts, financial data, news and analysis for global markets. Customizable technical indicators available.
- Yahoo Finance - Easy to use historical price charts with basic technical indicators and ability to download data. Covers global equities, indices, forex, commodities etc.

Make the most of these resources to deeply internalize concepts and enrich your understanding. Wishing you the very best in your stock market learning journey!

Yours in Learning,
Abhishek Parihar

# DEDICATION

To my friends,

In the crucible of life, true colors emerge. To those who stood with me in my darkest hours, you are my beacons of light. When I was on the precipice, you held me steady, and for that, you hold a place in my heart forever.

And to those who, in the days of plenty, chose to take advantage and left me to face my own trials, your actions etched indelible lessons in my soul. You reminded me that in self-reliance, true strength emerges.

This dedication is a testament to the intricacies of human relationships, the strength to endure, and the power to transform adversity into triumph.

With sincerity,

Abhishek Parihar

# ACKNOWLEDGMENTS

In the creation of **"Value Investing Essentials: Principles, Strategies, and Insights,"** I owe a debt of gratitude to:

The students who came distraught after losing their fortunes based on tips, habit of investing and trading without stop loss and investing without knowledge.

My unyielding friends, who stood by me in my darkest moments.

Those whose actions inadvertently became powerful lessons of resilience.

My wife and daughter, who I have not seen for a year, yet remain my unwavering source of strength.

To the readers, your presence in this journey is my greatest honor.

With sincere thanks,

Abhishek Parihar

# INDEX

# CHAPTER 1 - Introduction to the Indian Stock Market

## 1.1 Introduction

As an experienced trader and market enthusiast in India, I have had the privilege of participating in and observing the dynamic Indian stock markets over the past decade. In this chapter, I provide a comprehensive overview of the Indian share trading landscape - its history, governing bodies, prominent exchanges, popular brokerages, and essential account types.

The origin of stock trading in India dates back to the late 19th century during British rule. In 1875, the first stock exchange was established in Mumbai known as 'The Native Share & Stock Brokers Association'. It had only a handful of brokers trading a few stocks. Over the next century, this evolved into the Bombay Stock Exchange (BSE) which was formally constituted in 1957.

The 1990s were a pivotal period in the transformation of the Indian capital markets. Until then, trading was done through an open outcry system. The screen-based electronic trading was first introduced in 1994 at the NSE or National Stock Exchange, based in Mumbai. This ushered in tremendous efficiency, speed and transparency. Screen-based nationwide trading complemented the economic liberalization of the early 1990s.

Today, the NSE and BSE are the two leading stock exchanges in India accounting for the majority of trading volume. The NSE is the largest stock exchange with a total market capitalization of over $3 trillion. It offers trading across multiple asset classes including equities, debt, derivatives, currency and commodities. The BSE or Bombay Stock Exchange is the oldest exchange founded in 1875. It has a market capitalization of $2 trillion.

Let's look at the key governing bodies and regulatory institutions in the Indian capital markets:

- **SEBI - The Securities and Exchange Board of India** established in 1992 is the apex regulatory body for securities and commodity market regulation in India. SEBI enforces rules and regulations and protects the interests of investors. All intermediaries like exchanges, brokers, and merchant bankers come under SEBI's purview.

- **NSE - The National Stock Exchange of India** was incorporated in 1992 by leading institutions to provide nationwide online equities trading. It introduced electronic screen-based trading and ensured speed and efficiency of trades.

- **BSE - Formerly known as the Bombay Stock Exchange** founded in 1875, it is the oldest stock exchange in India. It provides an efficient and transparent market for trading various types of securities.

- **CDSL and NSDL - The Central Depository Services Limited and National Securities Depository Limited.** These depository institutions maintain and service electronic records of securities transactions and holdings.

For trading in stocks, investors need to open a Demat account and trading account with SEBI-registered intermediaries. The three types of accounts are:

1. **Demat Account** - This holds all the shares and securities in electronic or dematerialized format. Held with depository intermediaries like CDSL/NSDL.
2. **Trading Account** - Used to place buy/sell orders for shares. Held with brokerage firms and trading members.
3. **Bank Account** - Used to transfer funds to/from trading account for buying/selling shares.

Now let's look at some of the top stock brokerages in India that provide access to the exchanges:

- **Zerodha** - Leading discount brokerage known for its low brokerage charges, advanced trading platforms and digital tools. Very popular among DIY retail traders.
- **Upstox** - Fast growing discount broker known for its intuitive Pro trading platforms, minimalistic mobile app interface and quick account opening process.
- **5paisa** - Provides discounted commissions and a technology-focused trading platform with insightful tools. Owned by IIFL.
- **Angel Broking** - Full-service broker with excellent customer service, research services and good network of offline branches across cities.
- **ICICI Direct** - Stock trading arm of ICICI bank

providing 3-in-1 accounts and integration of demat, trading, banking.

- **HDFC Securities** - Leading brokerage service from HDFC bank with strong research reports and advisory services.
- **Kotak Securities** - Top broker by Kotak Mahindra Bank offering online trading and investment services on web and mobile.

The typical process for an Indian investor to start trading involves opening a Demat account and trading account, transferring funds into the trading account, and finally placing buy/sell orders on the NSE or BSE exchanges via their brokerage platform. Advancements in technology have made the account opening and trading processes seamless and convenient through digitization.

I hope this overview provides a good understanding of the origins of the Indian stock market, its exchanges, regulators, account types, and popular brokers. Equipped with this foundational knowledge, new investors and traders will be well-prepared to dive deeper into trading and investing. In the next section, we will look at the different types of trading in India.

⊢ΩΩΩΩΩΩΩΩΩΩΩΩΩΩΩΩΩΩΩΩΩΩ⊣

## 1.2 Types of Trading

Having set up the necessary trading accounts, let's explore the various mechanisms and platforms available for trading in the Indian share markets.

Broadly, trading can be classified based on order type, duration, and instrument.

## 1. Delivery Trading

Delivery-based trading involves buying shares and holding them for longer durations. The delivery of shares happens when you buy and hold the shares in your demat account instead of intraday square off. When you place a delivery order, the broker finalizes the transaction in the market and credits the shares to your demat account.

Delivery positions are held for the long-term to benefit from price appreciation over weeks, months or years. Traders opt for delivery to build long-term portfolios of stocks and mutual funds. Delivery-based investing requires thorough research and analysis to choose stocks of companies with good fundamentals, growth prospects and financial strength.

## 2. Intraday Trading

Intraday trading involves buying and selling shares within the same trading session, without carrying forward positions to the next day. Traders have to square off intraday positions before the market closes with the goal of profiting from intraday price movements and volatility in stocks.

This type of momentum trading requires a higher risk appetite as you aim to capitalize on smaller price fluctuations over the course of hours. Traders need to have thorough technical and chart analysis skills for successful intraday trading. You have greater leverage but the risk of losses is also higher if share prices move against your intraday bets.

### 3. Futures Trading

Equity futures contracts are derivative instruments where two parties agree to transact in an equity share at a future date and pre-decided price. It allows traders to gain leveraged exposure to underlying stocks without paying the full price.

For instance, Reliance Industries futures contract expiring in one month may have a lot size of 500 shares and trade at Rs 2400 per share. But you only have to pay a margin of say 10% i.e. Rs 120,000 to control the position and benefit from the price movements of RIL shares.

Futures are used for short-term trading and hedging. Day traders execute intraday strategies in equity futures for the high leverage. Positional traders hold futures for short periods to benefit from expected price movements. Hedgers use futures to mitigate risk in cash equities by taking opposite positions.

### 4. Options Trading

Options give buyers the right but not the obligation to buy (Call Option) or sell (Put Option) the underlying share at the strike price on expiry date. Buyers pay a premium upfront to gain this right from sellers who collect this premium.

For example, you buy 1 monthly Reliance 2400 Call Option by paying Rs 100 premium. If RIL trades above Rs 2400 on expiry, you can exercise the right to buy it at Rs 2400 and gain the difference. Else the option expires worthless.

Options trading requires understanding of concepts like spot price, strike price, premium, expiration date, and option Greeks like delta, gamma, theta. Options are used for directional trading, hedging and income strategies.

## 5. Currency Derivatives

The currency derivatives market includes currency futures and options contracts on Indian rupee and cross-currency pairs like EUR-INR, USD-INR. These instruments allow traders to hedge, arbitrage and speculate on currency rate fluctuations.

For example, an exporter can hedge dollar receivables by taking long positions in USD-INR futures contracts and benefit from rupee depreciation. An importer on the other hand can hedge costs by going short on the contracts.

## 6. Commodity Trading

Commodities like gold, silver, crude oil, natural gas, cotton, pepper etc. are traded on exchanges through futures contracts. This allows producers, end users and traders to hedge risk and speculate on commodity price volatility.

For instance, MCX gold futures allow jewelry makers

to hedge raw material costs. Traders bet on gold price movements to profit from global uncertainties. One can diversify portfolio beyond just equities by trading commodities.

## 7. Algorithmic Trading

This involves using advanced computer programs with complex algorithms to automate trading strategies. Algo trades are executed at high speeds, frequency and accuracy to capitalize profitable opportunities.

Algorithms can monitor markets based on technical indicators, trends, news events etc. and place orders even faster than humans to gain a competitive edge. While algo trading requires expertise, retail investors can also automate simple strategies.

Apart from the above order types and instruments, exchanges like NSE and BSE offer other variants like bracket order, cover order, after market order etc. based on price condition, disclosure, validity etc.

Now let's look at the key platforms available for trading in India:

- **Trading Terminals** - Desktop trading software like ODIN, NOW, NEST and DEAL provided by brokers for order placement and market data feeds.
- **Web Trading Platforms** - Browser-based platforms like ICICI Direct, Upstox Pro Web allow online trading without downloading software.

- **Mobile Apps** - Android & iOS apps like Zerodha Kite, Angel Broking, Groww provide intuitive stock trading apps for smartphones.
- **Robo-Advisory Platforms** - Automate mutual fund investing based on goals, risk appetite and enable passive hands-free investing.
- **Technical Analysis Software** - Desktop tools like MetaStock, Amibroker, TickQuest with TA indicators, charting and scanning features.

The typical stock investing lifecycle involves identifying the trading objectives, appropriate segment, conducting market research, opening suitable accounts, utilizing advanced trading platforms and applying prudent risk management. Technology has made trading seamless across web and mobile for today's digital savvy investors.

⊢ΩΩΩΩΩΩΩΩΩΩΩΩΩΩΩΩΩΩΩΩΩΩ⊣

## 1.3 Getting Started with Stock Trading

Now that we have understood the stock market structure and types of trading available, let's look at the step-by-step process for an investor to start trading in Indian equities.

- **Self-Analysis:** Assess investment goals and risk tolerance. Define the trading style - long-term or intraday, fundamental or technical, options vs cash, etc. This shapes account and platform choices.

Begin by clearly defining your investment objectives, time horizon and risk tolerance. This shapes the appropriate trading style and segments to focus on. Are you looking for long term wealth creation or short-term trading gains? Do you want to trade frequently intraday or invest for months/years? Can you stomach high risk with futures and options or prefer low risk delivery trading?

Based on your answers, you can choose between long-term buying, intraday trading, options trading etc., and select suitable trading platforms and brokerages. Realistically assess how much loss you can afford to incur from your capital. Define stop losses diligently

*""Amidst the tempest of the Indian stock market, a lone sentinel rises. Unyielding, unswayed, they heed no counsel but their own. In this solitary pursuit, fortunes are hewn, unfurling a saga of self-reliance that sends shivers through the marrow of every dreamer, reminding all that true mastery emerges from within, not from the echoes of others."*

**-Abhishek**

- **Demat Account Opening:** Open a demat account with CDSL/NSDL affiliated brokers like Zerodha, ICICI, HDFC etc. Submit KYC documents and fill the account opening form online or offline. Account gets opened in 1-2 days.

A Demat or dematerialized account in India is used to hold all bought shares and securities in electronic form. The account is opened with depository institutions - NSDL or CDSL. They allot a unique Demat account number. Leading depository participants include brokers like ICICI, HDFC, Kotak, Zerodha etc.

Here is the process to open a Demat account:

- ✓ Select a broker and fill up the account opening form online or offline along with required documents.
- ✓ Submit PAN card copy, address proof, passport photo, bank account details to the broker for KYC.
- ✓ Authorize the account using e-sign or physical signature as per type of account - online or offline.
- ✓ The broker verifies documents and shares application with the depository institution.
- ✓ On approval, they will allot a unique Demat account number to identify and credit share holdings.
- ✓ Obtain your User ID, login credentials and setup online access on the broker's portal.
- ✓ The account gets opened within few days. Download the depository statements periodically to track holdings. Leading brokers charge nominal annual maintenance charges for Demat account.

- **Trading Account Opening:** Open an equities trading account with a stock brokerage firm of your choice. Submit UCC, PAN, bank details, digital signature for online approval. Offline account opening may require in-person verification.

A share trading account is required for placing buy and sell orders for stocks and derivatives. It is linked to your Demat account, bank account and trading platform. Here are the steps:

- ✓ Choose a SEBI registered stock brokerage firm like Zerodha, Upstox, 5paisa, Angel Broking etc.
- ✓ Fill the trading account opening form and submit PAN, ID proof, residence proof, bank details, Demat account number etc.
- ✓ Authorize using digital signatures for online account opening or in-person verification if offline.
- ✓ The documents are verified by the brokerage house for KYC compliance with adequate due diligence.
- ✓ On approval, they allocate a unique trading account number. Login details are sent via email and SMS.
- ✓ Fund the new account via netbanking or UPI and start trading once formalities are completed. Top up with more capital as required.

- ✓ Ensure to check regulations, fee structure and trading platforms before zeroing in on a suitable brokerage.
- **Funding the Accounts:** Transfer funds to the trading account via NEFT/RTGS, netbanking or using UPI from supported banks. Ensure sufficient balance for trading margin requirements.

Transfer adequate capital into the trading account as per intended trading size and segments. Funding avenues:

- ✓ NEFT/RTGS or cash/cheque deposits directly into the trading account if supporting documents provided earlier.
- ✓ Netbanking - Add trading account details to your bank portal and transfer funds easily.
- ✓ UPI Apps - Use BHIM, PhonePe, PayTM, GPay to directly transfer funds from bank to trading account seamlessly.
- ✓ Keep surplus funds only in trading account and withdraw profits periodically to save on debit interest.
- **Install Trading Software:** Download the brokerage's trading platform on your desktop/mobile devices. For instance, Zerodha Kite, Angel Broking App, Upstox Pro. Understand the interface and features.

Brokers offer desktop and mobile trading platforms to

place and track your orders:

Desktop software like ODIN, NOW, EXE etc. have advanced charting, analytics and order management features. Mobile apps provide convenience of trading on the go.

- For Zerodha, install Kite desktop trading terminal and Kite mobile trading app.
- For Upstox, install its Pro Web trading platform or mobile app.
- For Angel Broking, install Angel BEE terminal and Angel Speed Pro app.
- Learn to use order entry, watchlists, charts, positions, funds and reports on these platforms effectively.
- **Learn Trading Basics:** Understand order types - limit order, market order, stop loss etc. Learn to read charts, financial statements, ratios. Read trading books and education material provided by the broker.

Learn how to place basic buy and sell orders:

- Limit Order - To buy/sell stock at set price or better. Specify a limit price.
- Market Order - To buy/sell immediately at the current market price shown.
- Stop Loss Order - To exit position and cap loss if the price reaches trigger point.

Understand order attributes like quantity,

disclosed/undisclosed qty, validity etc. and trading segments like delivery, intraday, futures etc.

- **Paper Trading:** Practice mock trading using virtual money to experience the real market environment without risking real capital. Build strategy skills.
    1) Paper trade for 1-2 months before live trading to understand practical nuances without real loss risks.
    2) Practice placing varieties of orders across segments to gain confidence.
    3) See order execution, positions, holding list, margins to experience real platform features.
    4) Participate in simulated intraday and positional trades end-to-end to know trading lifecycle.
- **Start Small:** _Begin actual trading with small position sizes in cash segment. Book small profits and losses to see practical results before scaling up._

Once familiar with account setup, order types and paper trading, start live trading slowly:

- Begin with small position sizes of just 1-2 shares on a delivery basis. Book small profits of Rs. 2-5% initially and Put Strict Stop Losses.
- Focus only on one or two large-cap stocks like Reliance, Infosys, and HDFC Bank for

simplicity initially.

- Keep maximum initial capital exposure below Rs. 10,000 per trade.
- Target daily profit of around Rs. 100-200 to start with. Increase amounts gradually.
- Manage risk well. Book small losses if stop loss triggers instead of hoping for reversals.

- **Leverage Tools:** Use screeners, chart patterns, price alerts, trading view charts etc. to gain trading edge. Subscribe to research services if required.

Analyze trading performance periodically:

- Review strategy effectiveness - is it working consistently or just by chance?
- Identify mistakes - wrong entry/exit timing, inadequate risk-reward trade-off etc.
- Maintain trading journal detailing each trade rationale, what went right or wrong.
- Continuously refine strategy taking cues from losses and successes. Develop robust thought processes.
- Set new incremental daily targets and position size limits and upgrade periodically.
- **Review and Refine:** Analyze your trading performance - losses, gains, mistakes to continuously refine strategy. Maintain trading journal and discipline.

Now let's understand the step-by-step process for executing an actual trade:

- **Market Analysis:** Based on trading style study market trends, company results, and technical levels before taking a position.
- **Funds Check:** Ensure sufficient margin is available in trading account for intended trades.
- **Order Placement:** Use trading platform to place buy/sell order for stock with details like price, quantity, order type.
- **Order Matching:** Order reaches stock exchange electronically and matches bid/ask prices as per order matching rules.
- **Trade Confirmation:** On successful match, broker confirms trade execution via order book and trade log on platform.
- **Settlement:** Buy shares settle in demat account. Funds get deducted for buy trades and added for sells.
- **Square off:** If intraday, close position with reverse trade before market closes to book profits. Carry overnight for delivery.
- **Holding:** For delivery trades, keep monitoring price action and fundamentals till exit target is reached.
- **Exit:** Finally, close position by selling shares on reaching profit objective or stop loss trigger.
- **Performance Review:** Analyze strategy effectiveness, mistakes post exiting the trades and trades.

Now let's look at some best practices for efficient trading:

1) Start with single segment like cash or futures to gain experience before trading multiple instruments.
2) Initially only take up to 1-2 trades per day to get a hang of the practical aspects and manage risk.
3) Focus on the profitability of trades rather than volume. Look for higher win rates and risk-reward payoff.
4) Don't chase losses or go beyond the planned maximum loss for a day. Stick to stop loss diligently.
5) Maintain adequate margin requirements in trading accounts and monitor open positions regularly.
6) Invest time upfront in honing trading and risk management skills before committing large capital.
7) Take smart risks only after factoring in affordability and diversification of the overall portfolio.
8) Use technology effectively - trade online via desktop and mobile, alerts, and analysis tools. But avoid overtrading.
9) Keep emotions aside. Don't let fear or greed impact disciplined trading. Don't take revenge trades.

***"Stop Loss: The Guardian of Every Trader's Journey. If you're unwilling to embrace its wisdom, then halt here. Donate this book to a local library, for true mastery in the stock market***

**_begins with the discipline of protecting your gains and minimizing your losses._**"

**- Abhishek**

The learning curve can seem steep initially. But with a structured approach, robust risk management, and exploitation of technology, investors can gain expertise and operate efficiently in the markets. Developing the right trading mindset and thought processes takes time and experience. Patience and perseverance eventually help succeed.

## _"Trading Requires Discipline"_

Follow these best practices for smooth trading:

- Adopt a structured approach instead of ad-hoc trades. Plan your trades and trades your plan.
- Stick to your strategy with discipline and don't sway with emotions like fear or greed.
- Maintain adequate margins upfront for all open positions and for trading continuity.
- Don't chase losses if a trade goes wrong. Stick to defined stop loss.
- Keep stop losses modest initially. Book small losses, ride winners for bigger profits.
- Don't take excessive risks beyond your affordability at early stages.
- Use trading safeguards like price alerts, automatic square offs to manage risk.

PROTECT YOUR
MONEY
SAFETY FIRST.USE
STOPLOSS
OTHERWISE THE RESULTS CAN BE DEVASTATING

# Chapter 2 - Fundamental Analysis

## 2.1 Introduction

Fundamental analysis is an investing approach that involves holistically analyzing a company's financial health and business prospects in order to determine its intrinsic value and investment worthiness. As Benjamin Graham, the father of value investing stated, "In the short run, the market is a voting machine, but in the long run, it is a weighing machine." Fundamental analysis aims to make use of the 'weighing machine' characteristic of markets.

Unlike technical analysis which relies solely on studying price charts and patterns, fundamental analysis dives deeper into financial statements, competitive landscape, industry outlook, management quality and macroeconomic factors to uncover a stock's true intrinsic value based on the company's business fundamentals. The key tools used are financial ratios, valuation models, due diligence and common sense principles.

The goals of fundamental analysis are multifold - to identify undervalued stocks trading below intrinsic value, to determine overvalued stocks trading at premium unwarranted by financials, and to assess the long term investment merits and risks of a business. Fundamental analysis requires developing a thorough understanding of the company's financial reports, principally the balance sheet, income statement, cash flow statement and shareholding pattern. A granular analysis is conducted using ratios like P/E, P/B, debt-to-equity, EPS growth etc. to value companies and compare peers.

Several valuation models are employed like discounted cash flow analysis, relative valuation multiples of peers, earnings yield models and asset-based models. While quantitative factors form a crucial piece, qualitative aspects like management quality, competitive advantages, growth runway and industry prospects are equally analyzed to paint a holistic picture. Risks are evaluated through sound frameworks by identifying red flags, reading between the numbers and through prudent judgement.

For instance, high debt, creative accounting practices, corporate governance issues, bloated valuations relative to fundamentals, regulatory interference, disruption threats and macroeconomic challenges can be potential risks. In essence, fundamental analysis aims to minimize losses by avoiding risky, poor quality businesses. While time consuming, it offers the benefit of evaluating businesses through an in-depth, first principles lens.

Warren Buffet and Charlie Munger are considered the paragons of fundamental investing. Their key tenets involve evaluating owner earnings, competitive moats, management ability and margin of safety. Case studies of marquee investors like Rakesh Jhunjhunwala provide insights into their thought process, principles and successful stocks backed by diligence. Common sense, patience and tuning out the market noise are core virtues. Valuation guides projected returns but price action decides entry-exit timings. Concentrated portfolios backed by highest conviction ideas based on detailed analysis typically outperform diversified portfolios without an analytical edge.

Fundamental analysis has evolved significantly from the early 20th century when Ben Graham first developed and fine-tuned the approach. Computing power, databases and electronic content have made analyzing voluminous company filings effortless today. Data mining tools provide powerful analytical capabilities to even retail investors. Creative destruction means fundamental clues need to be derived even from unconventional sources beyond regulatory filings like social media chatter, reviews, web traffic of companies.

Big data analytics and machine learning are increasingly augmenting aspects of fundamental investing. But human oversight, prudence and judgment remains crucial while incorporating these technologies. Fundamental investing in dynamic Indian markets requires continuous learning and development of frameworks tailored to capitalize on local investor behavior and trends. The evolution of business models also means constantly adapting valuation metrics.

In summary, fundamental analysis rewards the patient, analytical and prudent investor willing to put in hard yards analyzing companies rather than chasing market momentum. It attempts to minimize risk while maximizing returns through diligent research. In Ben Graham's words, "You are neither right nor wrong because the crowd disagrees with you. You are right because your data and reasoning are right." This timeless wisdom underscores the essence of fundamental investing. In the forthcoming sections, we shall explore the concepts, tools and techniques of fundamental analysis in detail with illustrative examples.

├ Ω Ω Ω Ω Ω Ω Ω Ω Ω Ω Ω Ω Ω Ω Ω Ω Ω Ω Ω Ω Ω Ω ┤

## 2.2 Understanding Financial Statements

Financial statements are the bedrock for conducting fundamental analysis on companies. They act as the raw data inputs which need to be carefully studied, interpreted and analyzed to evaluate financial health, unearth trends and derive insights into the business. The three key components of a company's financial statements are:

1) Balance Sheet
2) Income Statement
3) Cash Flow Statement

Along with these, the Shareholding Pattern is also crucial. Let's examine each statement in detail:

### 1. <u>Balance Sheet</u>

The balance sheet provides a snapshot of a company's financial position at a point in time, typically the end of a quarter or financial year. It summarizes a company's assets, liabilities and shareholder equity. As the name suggests, it balances -

<u>Assets = Liabilities + Shareholder's Equity</u>

**Assets** denote resources controlled by the company as a result of past transactions and events from which future economic benefits are expected to flow to the entity. Liabilities denote financial obligations that the entity owes to external parties. Shareholder's equity is the residual interest in assets after deducting all liabilities.

**Assets** and **Liabilities** are further classified into current and non-current. Current means expected to be realized or settled within 12 months. Non-current means beyond 12 months.

Key Components of Balance Sheet:

- **Current Assets** - Cash & equivalents, inventories, trade receivables, short-term loans & advances given by the company. High current ratio indicates good liquidity position.
- **Non-Current Assets** - Tangible fixed assets like property, plant & equipment, capital work in progress. Intangible assets like goodwill, patents, trademarks, long term investments and loans made by the company.
- **Current Liabilities** - Short term debt, account payables, wages payable, taxes payable, dividend payable, portion of long term debt maturing within 12 months. High current ratio and low current liabilities signify good short term financial health.
- **Non-Current Liabilities** - Long term debt obligations, deferred tax liabilities, long term provisions like retirement benefits, lease obligations. High proportion indicates possible risk of excessive interest burden affecting profits.
- **Shareholder's Equity** - Share capital + Reserves and Surplus together constitute Shareholder's Equity and indicate capital attributable to owners. Reserves include securities premium,

retained earnings, capital reserves. Higher Shareholder's Equity denotes lower external liabilities dependence.

The interplay between various balance sheet components determines financial stability. While interpreting the sheet, review liquidity position using working capital ratio. Check capital structure ratios like debt to equity. Assess asset turnover cycle using accounts receivables and inventory turnover. Compare historical trends and peer ratios to detect anamolies.

## 2. <u>Income Statement</u>

Also called profit and loss statement or P&L, the income statement summarizes income and expenses of the company over a period, typically quarterly or annually. It shows the company's revenue sources and expense items leading up to net earnings available to shareholders.

Key Components:

- **Revenue** - Earned from the main business operations and other operating income like investment dividends. Growth indicates rising sales and customer base.
- **Cost of Goods Sold** - Direct costs attributable to producing the sold goods or services like raw material costs. Lower COGS to Revenue ratio is better.
- **Gross Profit** - Revenue minus COGS. Higher gross profit ratio indicates greater pricing power and efficiency.

- **Operating Expenses** - Indirect expenses for operating the business - employee costs, sale & marketing costs, rent & utilities, insurance etc. Rising faster than revenue means cost issue.
- **Operating Profit** - Gross Profit minus operating expenses. Higher operating profit ratio signals stronger core business profitability.
- **Non Operating Items** - Other income like interest, sale of assets etc. Other expenses like interest costs.

- **Tax** - Provision for current and deferred taxes. Lower effective tax rate may signal tax optimization steps.
- **Net Profit** - PAT - Profit after tax attributable to shareholders. Rising PAT growth trajectory indicates profitability and prospects.

Review trends in PAT, operating profit ratios vs competition. Break up operating costs into finer categories for deeper analysis. Look for unusual or very high expenses. Tax optimization and creative accounting practices may inflate profits on paper temporarily.

### 3. <u>Cash Flow Statement</u>

While the income statement shows profits and losses, cash flow indicates actual cash generated and used by the business during the year. Cash transactions may differ from accrual accounting profits/losses.

**Cash Flow Statement sections:**

- ### Cash from Operating Activities:

Net Profit -> Non-cash adjustments like depreciation -> Changes in working capital -> Cash from Operations

Higher net cash from operations indicates the fundamental business is generating cash. Growing faster than net profits signals efficiency.

- ### Cash from Investing Activities:

Investments made in long-term assets like property, acquisitions etc. <- Proceeds from sale of long term assets.

Consistently negative means company is deploying cash obtained from operations for future growth investment.

- ### Cash from Financing Activities:

Proceeds from equity issuance like IPOs, FPOs. <- Cash used for dividends, debt repayment, interest costs.

Net Financing cash flow should steadily reduce as maturing companies rely less on external capital over time.

Cash flow analysis reveals quality of profits. Cash flow upside divergence from profits signals aggressive revenue recognition or accounting gimmicks. Healthy cash conversion and utilization for growth investments denotes fundamentally sound business.

### 4. Shareholding Pattern

Shareholding pattern discloses the number and percentage stake of promoter and public shareholders. High promoter holding above 50% indicates their confidence and skin in the game. Steadily increasing public shareholding shows wider investor confidence.

Institutional investors' share signals their confidence. High retail shareholder percentage may mean investor hype. Review changes in shareholding percentages over years to detect trends - increasing promoter pledge is a warning sign. The extent of foreign shareholding indicates global investor interest.

Analyze together with trading volume data to gauge shorter term institutional activity. Sizeable investor stakes by competitors may be strategic. Overall, balanced shareholding structure and demonstrated trust of marquee investors is positive.

In summary, financial statements provide invaluable quantitative data for holistic fundamental analysis. But prudent interpretation coupled with common sense judgement is key to derive the right qualitative insights from the numbers. Financial ratios make data comparable across companies and time periods. We explore financial ratios next. Please feel free to provide your inputs on enhancing this overview of financial statements.

⊢ΩΩΩΩΩΩΩΩΩΩΩΩΩΩΩΩΩΩΩΩΩΩ⊣

## 2.3 Key Financial Ratios

While financial statements provide raw data, financial ratios enable insightful relative analysis using ratio analysis techniques. Ratios make financials comparable across different-sized companies and across time periods by controlling for scale. Analysts use ratios for peer benchmarking, trend analysis and to derive clues about financial health and operating efficiency.

Here are some key categories of financial ratios:

- **<u>Profitability Ratios</u>**

Profitability ratios measure the company's ability to generate profits relative to revenue, assets, equity and other benchmarks. Higher and rising margins signify pricing power and efficiency.

o *Gross Profit Margin = Gross Profit / Revenue*

Higher ratio indicates ability to sell at higher than cost price.

o *Operating Profit Margin = Operating Profit / Revenue*

Signals profitability of core business operations excluding non-operating income/expenses.

o *Net Profit Margin = Net Profit / Revenue*

Considers impact of taxation and non-operating items along with core business profitability.

o *Return on Assets (ROA) = Net Profit / Average Total Assets*

Shows % earnings generated from total assets deployed, asset utilization efficiency.

o *Return on Equity (ROE) = Net Profit / Average*

*Shareholder's Equity*

Reveals % return delivered to shareholders on their equity investment in the company. High and rising ROE indicates robust business fundamentals.

- o *Earnings Per Share (EPS) = Net Profit to Equity Shareholders / Number of Equity Shares*

Important to value stocks and compare peers. Growth trajectory signals business prospects.

Evaluate profitability ratios relative to competition and own historical averages to assess financial performance. Analyze trends over last 5-10 years for sustained growth or early warning of issues.

- **Efficiency Ratios**

Efficiency ratios demonstrate company's efficacy in converting assets and liabilities into revenues and profits. It indicates faster turnaround and effective utilization of capital.

- o *Inventory Turnover = Cost of Goods Sold / Average Inventory*

Higher ratio signals faster inventory to sales conversion, lower holding costs.

- o *Days Inventory = Average Inventory / (Cost of Goods Sold / 365*

Lower days inventory outstanding signals inventory management efficiency.

    ○ *Receivables Turnover = Revenue / Average Receivables*

Shows efficacy of collecting dues from customers. Higher ratio is better.

    ○ *Days Receivables = Average Receivables / (Revenue / 365)*

Lower days receivables outstanding indicates tighter credit control on customers.

    ○ *Asset Turnover = Revenue / Average Total Assets*

Measures Revenue generating ability relative to assets. Higher ratio signals better asset utilization.

Evaluate inventory, receivables and assets turnover relative to sector averages and historical trends to assess operational efficiency in deploying capital.

- **<u>Leverage Ratios</u>**

Financial leverage or gearing ratios demonstrate proportion of debt funding relative to equity and ability to service debt obligations through earnings and cash flows.

    ○ *Debt/Equity Ratio = Total Debt / Total Equity*

Higher ratio indicates greater long term solvency risk due to high degree of debt relative to shareholder's equity.

    ○ *Interest Coverage Ratio = EBIT (Earnings before*

*Interest & Taxes) / Interest Expense*

Shows cushion available from earnings to cover interest costs. Higher ratio is better.

o *Debt Service Coverage Ratio = Net Operating Income / Total Debt Repayments*

Measures adequacy of operating cash flows to handle debt repayments. Higher ratio signals better debt serviceability.

Debt ratios need to be assessed in relation to industry/sector average leverage since capital intensity varies. Review trends over time. Interest coverage below 1.5x warrants caution.

o **Valuation Ratios**

Valuation ratios assess whether stock prices are overvalued, fairly valued or undervalued relative to financial performance and peers. They estimate downside/upside potential.

o Price to Earnings Ratio (P/E) = Market Price per Share / Earnings per Share

Widely used indicator to value stocks based on earnings. Compare with historical averages, industry averages and growth rates.

o Price to Book Value Ratio (P/B) = Market Price per Share / Book Value per Share

Measures valuation relative to net assets backing each share. Lower ratios signal undervaluation.

- *EV to EBITDA Ratio = Enterprise Value / Earnings before interest, taxes, depreciation and amortization*

- *Enterprise Value (EV) = Market Cap + Debt - Cash.*

Compares business valuation relative to operating cash profitability.

- *Price to Sales Ratio = Market Capitalization / Revenue*

Values stock based on revenue instead of earnings. Useful for pre-profit companies.

- *Dividend Yield = Dividend per share / Market price per share*

Measures income component of stock returns. Higher yields offer greater cushion during market declines.

No single ratio can determine overvaluation or undervaluation. A holistic approach weighing risk, growth, quality along with valuations is prudent. Historical averages provide a sound baseline for assessments.

- **<u>Quality Assessment Ratios</u>**

Business quality and financial strength is gauged through following ratios:

- *Working Capital = Current Assets - Current Liabilities*

Positive working capital signals short term liquidity. Ratio of over 1.5x considered good.

Interest coverage and Debt/Equity ratios discussed earlier also indicate quality.

- o *Current Ratio = Current Assets / Current Liabilities*

Coverage of near term obligations through liquid assets. Ratio of over 1.5x is comfortable.

High promoter group holding percentage in shareholding pattern indicates conviction.

A blend of valuation, debt and quality parameters offers an objective framework to assess business attractiveness for long term focused investors.

In summary, financial ratios offer a structured approach to analyze company fundamentals. Comparing ratios relative to past averages, peers, sector and benchmarks forms the crux of ratio analysis. Identifying inflection points in trends provides clues. Ratios have limitations if analyzed in isolation. But collectively, they provide invaluable inputs for investment decision making. Other useful ratios like cash flow to **EBITDA, return on capital employed (ROCE), fixed asset turnove**r etc. also provide insights for diligent investors.

⊢ΩΩΩΩΩΩΩΩΩΩΩΩΩΩΩΩΩΩΩΩΩΩΩ⊣

## 2.4 Company Analysis and Valuation Models

After a thorough study of financial statements and

ratios, we arrive at the crucial step in fundamental analysis - detailed company analysis and valuation. The goal is to determine business quality, growth prospects, and intrinsic value to identify investment-worthy companies. Here are some frameworks:

## **Business Model Evaluation**

Begin by developing an in-depth understanding of the company's business model and sources of competitive advantage using tools like Porter's 5 forces:

- Products/Services - Assess product portfolio, life cycle, pricing power, uniqueness, patents, brand equity
- Customers - Analyze target segments, retention rates, switching costs, distribution network
- Competition - Analyze direct and indirect competitors, market share trends, competitive advantages
- Suppliers - Evaluate bargaining power of suppliers, raw material risks
- Industry dynamics - Regulatory environment, disruption risks, macroeconomic factors

This helps assess sustainability of competitive advantages and longevity of growth runway.

## **Management Quality Analysis**

Company's direction is shaped significantly by its top leadership. Analyze management quality:

- Track record - Review performance, execution, integrity under current leadership
- Capital allocation - Assess capital investment

decisions taken and returns generated

- Communications - Do leaders articulate vision, strategy clearly? Are they transparent with facts?
- Innovation - Have new products, processes, technologies been launched successfully?
- Corporate governance - Is there sufficient independence, minority shareholder representation and protection?
- Succession planning - Is leadership pipeline robust? Is there over-reliance on founders?

Management's past performance and decision-making provide clues on the ability to steer future growth prudently and generate shareholder value consistently.

## Financial Health Assessment

Evaluate financial foundation and ratios on:

- Profitability - ROE, Margins, Earnings growth trajectory - rising or deteriorating?
- Leverage - Debt/Equity, Interest coverage - have debt levels become excessive?
- Liquidity - Working capital, Current ratio sufficient to manage short term needs?
- Efficiency - Inventory, receivables, asset turns - improving or worsening?

This determines if business fundamentals are strengthening or weakening over time.

## Quality of Profits Analysis

Review income statement and cash flows closely to assess:

- Revenue - Is growth driven by volume or price increases? Organic or acquisitions driven?
- Costs - Are major expense items rising faster than inflation and sector averages?
- Cash Flows - Do cash flows trails net profits? Are accrual profits getting converted to cash flows efficiently?

Evaluate these factors to gauge sustainability and cash profitability. Exercise caution if profits are driven majorly by accounting adjustments without cash flow conversions.

## Growth Runway Assessment

Analyze growth outlook based on:

- Market size - Assess market potential and penetration. Is market leadership increasing?
- Innovation - New products in pipeline to drive future revenues?
- Operating leverage - Can fixed costs be spread across higher revenue? Margin expansion potential?
- Financial leverage - Is debt taken only for capacity expansion and not overused?
- Long term investments - Are investments being made in capacities, technologies, platforms etc. to power future growth?

Higher profitability coupled with reinvestment for growth indicates a wider growth runway.

## Macroeconomic Factors

Evaluate business risks and opportunities from:

- Economic growth environment - Expansion plans may require upbeat GDP environment
- Interest rate trends - Higher rates increase costs for leveraged companies
- Commodity price risks - Raw material costs tied to volatile commodities?
- Currency fluctuations - For exporters and importers, forex trends are key
- Government policy - Changes in laws, taxes, incentives impact businesses
- Global geo-political risks - Trade wars, sanctions etc. affect global supply chains

Prudently assess how macroeconomic factors may influence future business performance.

## SWOT Analysis

Consolidate the strengths, weaknesses, opportunities and threats facing the company:

- Strengths - Competitive advantages, intangibles difficult to replicate
- Weaknesses - Disadvantages relative to competition, efficiency gaps
- Opportunities - Favorable industry trends, tailwinds, potential segments to target
- Threats - Risks that need mitigation - disruptions, adverse regulations, macro headwinds
- SWOT analysis summarizes qualitative company analysis concisely, highlighting areas requiring attention.

In summary, business model, management capability, financial health, quality of profits, growth outlook and macroeconomic analysis help assess business fundamentals thoroughly. This leads to the culmination - valuation.

## **Valuation Models**

Various models are employed to arrive at fair value estimates:

- **Discounted Cash Flow (DCF) Valuation**

DCF calculates present value of all expected future free cash flows based on projections of revenue, margins, capex, depreciation etc. divisor

▶ Valuation = $\sum$ FCFF / (1 + WACC) $^\wedge$ n

- FCFF = Free Cash Flow to Firm

- WACC = Weighted Average Cost of Capital

- n = period

DCF requires making prudent projections and using appropriate discount rates. More suitable for stable businesses.

▶ **Relative Valuation Models**

Relative valuation values companies based on ratios of comparable firms:

- Price to Earnings Ratio (P/E)
- Price to Book Value Ratio (P/B)
- Price to Sales Ratio (P/S)
- EV to EBITDA Ratio

Appropriate peer group selection is key. Companies in the same sector, size, and markets are preferable comparable. Relative valuation reveals whether stock is overvalued or undervalued relative to peers.

- **Asset Based Valuation**

Assets and liabilities are restated at fair market value and a ratio is applied:

▶ Price = Adjusted Net Assets x multiplier

Suitable for capital intensive sectors like infrastructure, real estate where assets form large portion of business value.

- EPS Valuation

Projected future EPS is multiplied by an appropriate P/E assigned based on growth potential:

▶ Price = EPS x P/E ratio

P/E ratios assigned based on industry maturity, competitive advantages, growth outlook.

No single model is perfect. Using a blend of relative valuation, DCF, EPS models offers a balanced approach. Weight operating and financial metrics appropriately based on business type. Identify overvalued or undervalued stocks relative to intrinsic value.

## Maruti Suzuki - Case Study

Let's apply the fundamental analysis steps discussed on an example company - Maruti Suzuki, India's largest carmaker:

- **Business model** - Leads passenger vehicles market with ~50% share. Competitive advantages from extensive service network, low cost of ownership, brand strength. Higher industry penetration potential.

- **Management** - Top management has steered company well with prudent expansion, good forex risk management. Proven execution track record.

- **Financial Health** - Strong profitability with ROE of ~15%. Low debt levels and high interest coverage. Good liquidity and working capital position. High efficiency in managing inventory and receivables.

- **Quality of Profits** - Revenues driven by volume growth in entry and mid-segment models. Raw material cost increases offset by operating leverage and price hikes. Cash flows closely mirror profitability trends.

- **Growth Runway** - India car penetration at ~3 per 1000 population offers huge runway for growth. Investments made to launch new models and expand capacities.

- **Macro factors** - India GDP growth crucial for demand. Commodity price inflation requires careful cost control. Expect long term structural growth story.

- **Valuation** - Trades at P/E of ~28x TTM EPS of

Rs. 87 per share. Justified based on leadership, prospects, RoE profile and historical multiples. Not cheap but reasonable valuation.

To summarize, Maruti Suzuki has a robust business model with strong financial health, experienced management and leadership position. Long term growth levers intact but being priced at slight premium. Periodic market corrections can offer opportunities for long term investors.

I hope these illustrations provide a good overview of applying structured fundamental analysis in practice.

⊢ΩΩΩΩΩΩΩΩΩΩΩΩΩΩΩΩΩΩΩΩΩΩΩΩΩ⊣

## 2.5 Case Studies of Fundamental Analysis on Indian Companies

By examining case studies, we can better understand how leading investors apply fundamental analysis principles in practice when researching companies. Let's review 4 Indian stocks analyzing their business models, financials, valuations and intrinsic value estimates:

### Infosys

- **Business Model**

  - o IT services pioneer serving global 2000 clients. Digital, cloud, AI capabilities.
  - o Strong management and talent pool. High client retention rates.
  - o Competes with TCS, Accenture, Wipro, Cognizant. Maintains industry-leading margins.

- **Financial Analysis**

  o Revenue USD 16.3 billion. Net Profit margin 22%, ROE 29%. Zero debt.
  o Excellent balance sheet strength. High current ratio 2.5x. Cash reserves USD 3.5 billion.
  o Revenue growth accelerated to 19.7%. Digital segment grew at 47%. Operating margins expanded.
  o Strong quality of earnings. Net cash from operations equals PAT. High cash conversion.

- **Valuation**

  o Trades at P/E ratio of 28x based on TTM EPS of Rs 58 per share. Forward P/E is 24x.
  o EV/EBITDA ratio is 20x, lower than historical average of 23x. Price/Book ratio is 10x.
  o Dividend payout ratio is 50-60%. Dividend yield 1.6%.

- **Intrinsic Value Estimate**

  o DCF model using 10% cost of equity: Intrinsic value works out to Rs 1,900 per share.
  o Relative valuation: Adjusted forward P/E of 22x for projected growth gives fair value of Rs 1,700 per share.

Recommend buy below Rs 1,500 for margin of safety. Promising pick for portfolio.

## Bajaj Finance

- Business Model

o Leading consumer finance NBFC with interest income across products like loans, credit cards.
o Network of 5,000+ partner locations. Customer base - 52 million.
o Competes with banks and NBFCs like HDFC, ICICI, Chola Finance.

- **Financial Analysis**

o AUM grew by 29% to Rs. 1.8 lakh crore. Net interest income rose by 31%.
o Net profit grew by 43% to Rs 5,200 crore. ROAE 29%, ROAA 4.7%.
o Strong asset quality with gross NPAs just 1.25%. Capital adequacy ratio of 28%.
o Leverage comfortable. Debt/Equity ratio 3.4x. Coverage ratios adequate.

- Valuation

o Trades at Price/Book ratio of 8.5x. P/E ratio of 73x seems elevated but earnings growth justifies premium.
o EV/EBITDA ratio is 18.5x.
o Healthy return ratios warrant higher multiples. But limit upside.

- **Intrinsic Value Estimate**

o DCF model with 15% cost of equity gives fair value of Rs 5,000 per share.
o Relative valuation with adjusted P/E of 45x gives intrinsic value of Rs 5,300 per share.

Recommend gradual accumulation below Rs 5,000 for long term gains.

## **Avenue Supermarts (D-Mart)**

- **Business Model**

  o Largest hypermarket retail chain with focus on value pricing and cost efficiency.
  o Stores located across metro and tier 2 cities. High penetration in western India.
  o Competes with retailers like Big Bazaar. Also unorganized Kirana stores.

- **Financial Analysis**

  o Revenue Rs. 11,000 crore with EBITDA margin at 9%. Net profit margin 6%.
  o High return ratios with ROE 32%, ROCE 45%. Low debt, Inventory turns 17x.
  o Stores expansion continuing at fast pace with target to reach 3,000 stores.
  o Negative working capital model. Cash conversion cycle very low at 2 days.

- **Valuation**

  o Trades at P/E ratio of 192x and P/B ratio of 15x indicating premium valuation.
  o EV/EBITDA ratio is at 64x. Market leader premium justified but limited upside.
  o Price/Sales ratio is 8.6x. Revenue and PAT grew at 24% and 23%.

- **Intrinsic Value Estimate**

  o DCF model with 12% cost of equity yields fair value estimate of Rs 3,200 per share.
  o Relative valuation of 140x adjusted P/E gives

intrinsic value of Rs 3,500 per share.

- o Recommend accumulation only on corrections closer to Rs 2,800 for margin of safety.

## **Titan Company**

- **Business Model**

- o Largest jewellery manufacturer and retailer with flagship brand Tanishq. ~6% market share.
- o Also leading watches, eyewear brands. Category leader in discretionary segments.
- o Retail network of 400+ Tanishq stores across 200 cities.

- **Financial Analysis**

- o Consolidated Revenue Rs. 27,700 crore. Jewellery segment 68% of sales.
- o ROE 27%, ROCE 43%. Margins expanded despite high gold prices with operating leverage.
- o Low debt with Debt/Equity ratio of just 0.11x. High interest coverage.
- o Inventory turns increased to 3.8x. Working capital requirements reducing gradually.

- **Valuation**

- o Titan trades at P/E ratio of 97x and P/B ratio of 28x factoring its category leadership and structural growth story.
- o EV/EBITDA ratio stands elevated at 55x. Price/Sales ratio is 12x.
- o Market premium justified only slightly given jewellery is a discretionary category unlike staples.

- **Intrinsic Value Estimate**

  o DCF model with 11% cost of equity gives fair value estimate of Rs 3,000 per share.
  o Relative valuation at 80x P/E yields intrinsic value of Rs 2,900 per share.

Recommend gradual accumulation on 10-15% corrections from current levels closer to Rs 2,400.

In summary, meticulous fundamental analysis reveals valuable insights into business quality, financial health, growth outlook and intrinsic value. While valuation guides investing decisions, accumulating high conviction stocks requires patience to buy at reasonable prices. Developing a sound analytical thought process takes time and experience.

# Chapter 3 - Technical Analysis

## 3.1 Introduction

Technical analysis is an investing approach that involves analyzing statistical trends gathered from historical price movements and trading volumes to identify patterns and predict future activity. It is based on the premise that while it is difficult to predict how fundamentals like earnings will play out, the disciplined investor can extrapolate useful clues from how the market has valued the stock in the past as revealed through price charts.

The key tools used are price action, chart patterns, technical indicators and other trading signals. Technical analysis does not aim to evaluate the intrinsic value of the business. Rather it focuses on studying price momentum, identifying support and resistance zones, analyzing trading volumes, gauging supply and demand dynamics and assessing sentiment.

The goal is to develop probabilistic insights into the potential future trajectory of stock price based on precedent market psychology revealed through the charts. The timeframes studied vary from very short durations like 1 minute for scalping trades to multi-year charts for deciphering long term trends. The ideologies guiding technical analysis have evolved from the pioneering work of Charles Dow around market trends and reversals to the principles on price action and volumes by Richard Wyckoff and broader concepts like Elliot Waves, Gann Angles etc.

In technical analysis, the adage "The trend is your

friend" underscores the importance of momentum. Technical analysts ride emerging trends through momentum strategies until key reversal signals are observed. The most basic yet powerful technical indicators are the moving averages which smooth out daily volatility and reveal underlying trends. The interplay between short term and long term moving averages provides trading signals like golden crossovers and death crosses to enter and exit positions.

Technical analysts extensively use candlestick charts to assess price patterns and reversal signs based on the visual shape, size and color of the candlesticks. Pure price action techniques involve visual chart reading skills to observe double tops, head and shoulder patterns, flag and pennant formations, support and resistance levels, breakouts and breakdowns. Volumes add further confirmation for trading signals and to gauge accumulation or distribution trends.

Oscillators like RSI, Stochastics track momentum while Bollinger Bands study volatility dynamics. Directional Movement Index quantifies price trend strength. MACD analyzes moving average convergence divergence to detect changes in momentum. Price-based indicators are further supplemented by statistics-driven signals. For instance, the Average Directional Index provides a numeric measure of trend strength and direction on a scale of 0 to 100.

Technical analysis techniques enable traders to

develop quantitative rule-based strategies which can be easily backtested and automated. Algorithmic trading strategies extensively employ technical indicators like support-resistance levels, moving average crossovers, price breakouts etc. to systematically generate entry and exit signals and capture short term trends across stocks and asset classes. The efficacy of technical trading systems can be evaluated through statistical measures like profit factor, Sharpe ratio and maximum drawdowns observed.

Critics argue that technical analysis is prone to overfitting on the past and may not work reliably in the future. But practitioners counter that human psychology tends to repeat itself and fall into similar patterns consistently. Technical analysis aims to capture this repetitive investor behavior by studying past precedents. Position sizing, risk management and combining technicals with a contextual understanding of fundamentals can enhance risk adjusted returns.

Technical analysis has proved its utility for short to medium term trading over multiple market cycles and asset classes. But mastering chart reading skills, gaining experience in identifying reliable patterns and developing robust trading systems takes significant practice and discretion. In dynamic Indian markets, technical traders need to adapt indicator parameters and techniques to suit local conditions. Just like driving, technical trading is a skill acquired through experience and presence of mind.

In summary, technical analysis offers a structured approach to decipher market psychology and position for short term opportunities. Though past performance may not guarantee future results, insightful technical traders can opportunistically capitalize on high probability setups while tightly controlling risks. In the forthcoming sections we will explore concepts, techniques and real-world trading strategies based on technical analysis.

⊦ΩΩΩΩΩΩΩΩΩΩΩΩΩΩΩΩΩΩΩΩΩΩΩΩ⊣

## 3.2 Chart Patterns

Chart patterns are recurring price formations that technical analysts interpret to identify trading opportunities. They reveal how other market participants are positioned and poised to trade. By analyzing price action contextually, traders aim to determine high probability trade entry and exit points. Let's examine the most common chart patterns.

### Support and Resistance

Support and resistance levels denote price zones where demand/supply dynamics change significantly. This results in the price reversing or pausing its upward/downward momentum each time it reaches these zones.

- **Support** - Prices stop falling and rebound up from this floor level as fresh demand emerges. Former resistance zones when broken become supports.

- **Resistance** - Prices struggle to rise past this ceiling level as supply increases. Former support levels when broken turn into resistance.

Traders buy near supports with stop loss below support. Short selling is done near resistances with stop loss above resistance. Price bouncing between support and resistance results in range bound movement. Breakouts from ranging markets occur when price sustains above/below support/resistance.

## Trends

Uptrends form when the market makes higher highs and higher lows. Downtrends take shape when the market registers lower highs and lower lows. Trading with the trend direction offers highest probability.

- **Uptrends** - Ideal to buy pullback dips from rising 20-day moving average. Book profits at potential resistances.
- **Downtrends** - Look to short sell bounces and rallies. Cover shorts at supports. Trailing stop loss to ride downtrend.
- **Trend reversals** are signaled when price breaches key support or resistance levels. Trend strength is assessed using ADX indicator. Sideways choppy markets lack a definitive trend.

## Moving Averages (MA)

MAs smooth out daily volatility revealing the underlying trend. Crossovers between short term and long term MAs signal change in momentum.

- **Bullish crossover** - Faster MA crosses above slower MA. Indicates uptrend acceleration.
- **Bearish crossover** - Faster MA drops below slower MA. Signals potential downtrend emergence.

The 20-50-200 day MAs are widely followed. Price bouncing between 20 and 50 day MAs signals range bound action.

## Candlestick Patterns

Candlesticks visually express range, open/close and movement. Candle color conveys bullish/bearish bias. Wicks show intraday volatility.

**Some key reversal signals:**

- **Hammer, Inverted Hammer** - Bullish signal when lower wick at least 2x body size. Inverted has upper wick.
- **Engulfing candle** - Bullish if body fully engulfs previous red candle. Bearish if engulfed by subsequent green candle.
- **Doji** - Neutral with opening and closing price same indicating indecision. Gaps up are bullish while gaps down are bearish signals.
- **Shooting star** - Upper wicks at least 2-3x body size. Potential bearish reversal signal.

Candlestick patterns offer visually intuitive entry points. But other indicators should confirm signals.

## Double Tops and Bottoms

Double top forms after upward move, two similar peaks reached as resistance blocks further upside. Indicates potential bearish reversal.

Double bottom forms after downward move, two similar troughs reach support area. Signals potential bullish resurgence.

Partial decline or rise between peaks/troughs validates pattern. Price breaks below/above neckline confirms reversal. Target measured by height. Stop loss on opposite side of neckline.

## Head and Shoulders (H&S)

A topping pattern signaling trend reversal from uptrend. Formed by:

- **Left shoulder** - Rally peaking, decline back to support
- **Head** - Renewed advance stopping at higher peak
- **Right shoulder** - Final advance stopping lower than head
- **Neckline support** break confirms bearish signal. Measured target - height of head subtracted from neckline break level.
- **Inverse H&S** is bottoming pattern signaling uptrend reversal in downtrends. Rules similar but inverted.

## Flags and Pennants

Continuation patterns signaling brief consolidation before preceding uptrend or downtrend resumes.

- **Bullish Flag** - Rectangular pattern forms after sharp rally. Breakout above flag signals continuation. Target - height of previous move upwards from breakout level.
- **Bullish Pennant** - Triangle shaped. Tightening pattern after big advance as trend gathers steam for next leg up. Trade in direction of Existing trend when consolidation breaks.

## Cup and Handle

A bullish continuation pattern forms like a U or rounded bottom cup. Handle forms through drifting sideways action before breakout above handle resistance and prior peak confirms uptrend resuming. Shows market accumulation.

Inverse or Inverted Cup and Handle forms during downtrends. Trade in direction of subsequent breakout from handle and rim resistance.

## Wedges

Wedges signal temporary indecision consolidations before forceful breakout or breakdown.

Rising wedge forms during uptrends. Break below lower wedge boundary turns market bearish. Short sell confirmed breakdowns.

Falling wedge forms during downtrends. Break above upper wedge boundary revives upside momentum. Buy confirmed breakouts.

## Channel Patterns

Prices oscillate between parallel trendlines signalling an established directional move.

- **Uptrend Channels** - Price bounces between rising lower trendline support and upper trendline resistance. Buy low in channel, sell high.
- **Downtrend Channels** - Short sell upper channel trendline resistance. Cover shorts at lower support trendline.

A breakout signals trend change. New channel may form with steeper/flatter gradient.

## Gaps

Gaps are empty spaces left on chart when opening price is significantly below/above previous close. Signify urgency in buyers or sellers.

- **Continuation Gap** - Occurs midway during established uptrend or downtrend. Continues trend direction.
- **Breakaway Gap** - Signals new trend start. Confirmed when gap doesn't get filled after subsequent move.
- **Exhaustion Gap** - Happens near trend ends as final burst of enthusiasm. Then u-turn follows. Filled quickly.
- **Common Gap** - Neutral significance and gets filled soon. Requires other indicators for trade signals.

Effective technical traders identify high probability

chart pattern formations taking the broader market structure and other indicators into account. Mastering visual pattern recognition through screen time and examples aids success.

Now let's examine example charts on prominent Indian stocks to illustrate analyzing real price action contextually:

## Reliance Industries (RIL) - Double Bottom

RIL downtrend from 2018 peak at Rs 1,100 made lower low forming first trough at Rs 875 in February 2020. Recovery was short-lived as Covid crash dragged prices lower again forming second trough at Rs 867 in March 2020.

This double bottom pattern coincided with positive divergence on RSI-14 indicator signaling bullish momentum building up. As neckline resistance of Rs 1,000 was taken out decisively in June 2020, it confirmed double bottom target of Rs 1,240 (height Rs 133).

Price steadily rose to hit target over the next 3 months. Traders entering on neckline breakout would have captured most of the upmove through end 2020. Stop loss below Rs 900 protected downside effectively.

## Infosys - Bullish Flag continuation pattern

During strong uptrend from March 2020 lows, Infosys formed a bullish flag pattern through August and September 2020 with tight range bound action between Rs 1,000 and Rs 1,100 acting as parallel trendlines.

The breakout above Rs 1,100 resistance on above average volumes in early October 2020 signaled resumption of uptrend as projected height of Rs 200 pointed to target of Rs 1,300.

Price rose steadily to hit target by end November 2020. Thus trading the bullish flag setup generated around 18% returns over 2 months. Maintaining stop loss below Rs 1,050 protected capital despite whipsaws.

## Titan Company - Head & Shoulders reversal

Titan formed a head & shoulders topping pattern from August to November 2019 as uptrend off the 2019 lows matured.

Left shoulder peak formed in August 2019 at Rs 1,300. The higher head topped out at Rs 1,340 in September 2019 forming higher high. The right shoulder made a lower high at Rs 1,310 in November 2019.

Neckline support at Rs 1,270 broke decisively in December 2019 confirming trend reversal. Measured target based on head height of Rs 80 projected move towards Rs 1,190. This played out over next few months.

Traders shorting the break of neckline support benefitted from 25% down move over the next quarter by closely managing trade with pinpoint stop loss.

## TCS - Falling Wedge pattern

TCS formed a falling wedge pattern from February to April 2022 during intermediate downtrend. Upper wedge resistance trendline connected lower highs while lower support connected higher lows.

Wedge support held above Rs 3,000 while lower highs formed under Rs 3,400 resistance. The breakout above wedge and horizontal resistance at Rs 3,400 in May 2022 on strong volumes confirmed downtrend ending.

Fresh uptrend gave opportunity for momentum traders to profit. Stop loss below Rs 3,300 protected capital against false signals while riding upside. Adding other indicators confirmed high probability setup.

Thus by contextual chart reading and combining patterns with volume and momentum oscillators, traders can improve trade success rates and risk-reward outcomes. Gaining experience through observations and screen time is key for expertise.

I hope these real market examples provide useful contexts for applying chart pattern analysis. Please feel free to suggest specific chart patterns or trading strategies you would like me to detail with illustrations. Will be happy to expand on technical concepts further.

⊢ Ω Ω Ω Ω Ω Ω Ω Ω Ω Ω Ω Ω Ω Ω Ω Ω Ω Ω Ω Ω Ω Ω Ω Ω ⊣

## 3.3 Technical Indicators

In addition to observing price action and patterns, technical traders rely extensively on indicators that mathematically transform price and volume data into trading signals. Indicators capture market dynamics like momentum, volatility and trend strength which is not visually apparent. Let's examine the most popular indicators:

## Moving Averages (MA)

Moving averages smoothen price action by taking average closing price over periods like 20, 50, 200 days. Crossovers signal momentum changes.

- **Bullish crossover** - Short term MA crosses above longer term MA indicating uptrend acceleration.
- **Bearish crossover** - Short term MA drops below longer term MA signalling potential downtrend.

Price bouncing between 20 and 50 day MA indicates rangebound action.

Traders buy breakouts above 20-50 day MAs in uptrends. In downtrends, short sell breakdowns below MAs.

## Relative Strength Index (RSI)

RSI measures speed and magnitude of directional price movements on a scale of 0 to 100.

Overbought above 70 indicates potential reversal lower. Oversold below 30 signals likely resumption of uptrend.

Divergence with price predicts trend changes. If price rises but RSI falls, expects weakness.

RSI boom and bust cycles work well when confirmed

with MAs. Buy oversold, sell overbought.

## **Moving Average Convergence Divergence (MACD)**

MACD depicts relationship between short term 12-day and long term 26-day exponential moving averages (EMA).

MACD line crossing above signal line indicates bullish momentum strengthening.

Bearish when MACD crosses below signal line.

Trade breakouts and breakdowns in direction of crossovers confirmed by higher volumes.

## **Bollinger Bands**

Bands encompass price movement based on standard deviation of 20-day simple moving average.

Price reaching upper band suggests overbought conditions. Price hitting lower band indicates oversold zone.

Bands expanding signals increased volatility. Contracting bands show reduced volatility.

Trade reversions to mean when price touches bands. Also breakouts during band contractions.

## **Average Directional Index (ADX)**

ADX measures strength of prevailing trend on scale of 0 to 100.

Values above 25 signals building trend strength. Above 50 indicates strong trend.

Trade with trend when ADX above 25. Avoid choppy conditions when ADX below 20.

## Stochastic Oscillator

Stochastics analyze where close price is in relation to high-low range over 14-period lookback.

Overbought above 80 predicts possible reversal. Oversold below 20 flags resumed uptrend.

Trade overbought/oversold readings showing divergence against price.

Now let's examine real trading examples applying these indicators:

## Infosys - 20-100-200 Moving Averages

During uptrends, Infosys consolidated and formed bases when price stayed above rising 20-day MA. Dips to middle band 50-day MA offered low risk buying opportunities.

Bullish crossover of 20-day above 100-day MA in May 2020 signaled momentum acceleration ahead. MA held as support on retests.

In downtrends, resistance formed when price capped below falling 20-day MA. Breakdowns below 50-day MA provided short sell signals.

## TCS - RSI Divergence

As TCS hit new high in Sept 2021, RSI formed lower high indicating waning momentum. This bullish divergence signaled potential trend change.

Price reversed lower in October 2021 just as projected by lagging momentum. RSI downturn below 50 confirmed weakness.

RSI forming higher low in Feb 2022 as price bottomed signaled positive momentum divergence. Buying opportunity was presented.

## Titan - MACD Crossover

Bullish crossover of MACD line moving above signal line in June 2020 after correction confirmed upside momentum revival.

Sustained trading above zero line indicated uptrend. Bearish crossover in Sept 2021 signaled distribution ahead. Change in market character was visually signaled by MACD.

## Asian Paints - Bollinger Bands

Narrowing of bands during April-May 2020 pointed to lowering volatility ahead. Sharp expansion of bands in June signaled trend start. Breakout above upper band presented long entry.

Reversion to middle band in August 2020 offered low risk entry. Trade in direction of bands by buying high and selling low.

Thus combining indicators provides high conviction signals. Use different timeframes - shorter for entry, longer for directional bias. Be adaptive to evolving market behavior.

## **Volume Analysis**

Volume adds important supporting evidence. Upside breakouts confirmed by high volumes signal conviction. High volume distribution days mark potential topping signs. Volume precedes price changes.

## **On Balance Volume (OBV)**

OBV tracks cumulative buying and selling volumes. Uptrends show rising OBV. Downtrends marked by falling OBV. Watch for divergences.

## **Accumulation-Distribution Line**

Tracks volume relative to price movements. Increases on days when price closes above midpoint of range. Declines when close below midpoint. Interpret divergences and trends.

Volume-based indicators must be analyzed with price action contextually to determine when institutional accumulation or distribution is occurring.

In summary, technical indicators quantify price action and momentum trends. Trading signals require confluence of:

- Indicator signals confirming each other
- Significant volume participation
- Conformity with overall market direction
- Favorable risk-reward

No single indicator works perfectly all the time. Price behavior and liquidity conditions vary across stocks and market phases. Adaptive usage combining chart reading skills aids success. Indicators should expand analysis, not trigger mechanical trades. I hope these illustrations offer useful contexts on applying indicators in real markets. Happy to expand on trading strategies combining technical factors. Look forward to your feedback.

⊢ Ω Ω Ω Ω Ω Ω Ω Ω Ω Ω Ω Ω Ω Ω Ω Ω Ω Ω Ω Ω Ω Ω ⊣

## 3.4 Trading Strategies

By combining different chart patterns, indicators and trading techniques, technical analysts develop rule-based strategies for entries, exits and risk management. Let's explore popular trading strategies:

### Breakout Trading

Breakouts occur when price closes decisively outside key support or resistance levels with high volumes. Significant upside/downside follow through movement is expected post breakout.

- **Upside breakouts** - Buy when price breaks above resistance zones like previous swing highs, trendlines, moving averages, chart patterns. Indicates rising momentum.
- **Downside breakouts** - Look to short sell when price breaks below key supports like recent swing lows, moving averages, trendline support. Suggests building downward momentum.

Have stop loss 3% below breakout price. Book partial

profits at 1:1, 1:2 risk-reward ratio. Trail remaining position with price momentum.

## Pullback Trading

Pullbacks refer to temporary minor corrections against the prevailing uptrend. Indicates bulls absorbing selling pressure.

Identify stocks in strong uptrends with series of higher highs and lows. Avoid choppy sideways markets.

Buy when pullback declines to rising 20-day moving average providing higher low entry.

Can also buy at 61.8% Fibonacci retracement level of latest swing move.

Keep wider stop at recent swing low. Book profits at next resistance zone, previous high or trailing behind price.

## Trend Trading

The adage "The trend is your friend" captures essence of trend trading. Trading in harmony with strong trend improves win rate.

- **Uptrend Trading:**

Look for stocks making series of higher highs and lows indicating solid uptrend.

Identify corrections to buy dominated by buyers. e.g. retest of previous breakout level acting as support.

Buy on pullback dips to rising 20 or 50-day moving average giving higher low entry.

Place initial wider stop below recent higher trough. Trail stop up with uptrend. Book profits at potential resistances.

- **Downtrend Trading:**

Short stocks making lower tops and lower bottoms denoting solid downtrend.

Sell short rallies up to falling 20 or 50-day moving average providing lower high exit.

Put initial wider stop above recent swing high. Trail stop down with downtrend. Cover shorts at possible supports.

Trade only in direction of strong trend identified using ADX above 25. Avoid countertrend trades which have lower success rate.

- **Momentum Trading**

Momentum traders aim to capitalize on accelerated price movements and strong trends as they emerge. Indicators like moving averages, MACD and RSI help time entries.

Identify stocks demonstrating bullish momentum with indicators like RSI moving above 50 or positive slope in MACD.

Enter breakouts from consolidations and chart patterns on high volumes.

Buy pullback declines to maintain exposure to uptrend. Avoid exiting prematurely.

Book profits systematically at next technical resistance. Trail stops up but give room for momentum to sustain.

Be flexible across timeframes. Ride winners for multi-week trends but cut losers quickly when momentum stalls.

- **Swing Trading**

Swing trading aims to capture gains from intermediate multi-week trends and swings in both directions by managing positions nimbly.

Use higher timeframe charts like daily and weekly to assess primary trend.

Identify tradeable swings and rotations on lower timeframes like hourly.

Enter on retracements and reversals at oversold/overbought extremes.

Book profits at technical levels, pivot points on lower timeframe. Protect positions with wide stops.

Be swift to cut losses. Let winners ride with tailing stops. Avoid overtrading and only take best 1-2 setups a week.

- **Combination Strategies**

Savvy traders develop strategies combining factors like:

- **Market phase** - Trending, rangebound, volatile
- **Timeframes** - Higher TF to identify bias, lower TF for entry
- **Chart patterns** - Confirming indicators required for high conviction
- **Watchlist filters** - ADX, volatility, liquidity, sectors
- **Risk management** - Size, wider stops, manage based on price action

No single perfect strategy. Adapt based on evolving market behavior by analyzing past trades. Consistently applying robust trading rules and risk management elevates performance.

Now let's examine some real chart examples in Indian markets:

- **Breakout Trading:**

Infosys breaking out above 9-month range in April 2020 from Rs 700 indicating start of strong uptrend.

Reliance Industries breaking above Rs 2,000 resistance in Sept 2020 fueling upward momentum.

- **Pullback Trading:**

HDFC Bank retesting April 2020 breakout level near Rs 1,000 providing buying opportunity with tight stop under recent swing low.

TCS pulling back to 20-day MA near Rs 3,150 during uptrend gave attractive risk-reward long entry in June 2022.

- **Trend Trading:**

Bajaj Finance in strong 2020-22 uptrend offered multiple buying opportunities on dips to 20-day MA.

She Shorting BPCL's steep downtrend from Jan 2022 high made sense with sells into counter-trend bounces near Rs 400 resistance.

In summary, technical traders develop rule-based strategies combining indicators with chart patterns while adapting to evolving market conditions. Patience and discipline in adhering to trading rules elevates win rates. Managing risk smartly ensures longevity in trading journey. Please feel free to suggest specific trading techniques or examples I can expand on further. Look forward to your feedback.

⊢ΩΩΩΩΩΩΩΩΩΩΩΩΩΩΩΩΩΩΩΩΩΩΩ⊣

## 3.5 Technical Analysis Examples on Indices and Stocks

Technical analysis techniques apply effectively to index and stock trading. Technicals allow traders to time entries and exits prudently by assessing risk-reward scenarios. Let's examine examples on the benchmark Nifty and Sensex indices and major stocks.

### Nifty Technical Analysis

Nifty 50 is the bluechip index with 50 large cap stocks representing about 65% market capitalization of NSE. Widely tracked by traders to gauge market momentum.

- **Uptrends and Downtrends**

During uptrends, Nifty makes series of higher highs and higher lows. 20-day MA acts as support on dips. RSI in bullish mode trading above 50.

In downtrends, index registers lower highs and lower lows. Look to sell rallies that get capped by falling 20-day MA. Oversold RSI near 30 signals potential reversal up.

- **Trading Ranges**

Nifty frequently trades rangebound between support and resistance boundaries.

Range trading strategies: Buy near support and sell at resistance. Trail stop below support in longs and above resistance on shorts. Play reversion to mean by selling highs and buying lows.

For breakouts: Initiate longs above resistance with stop under support. Enter shorts below support with stop at upper range boundary.

- **Moving Average Analysis**

Crossovers between 20, 50 and 200-day MAs signal change in trend.

Bullish when 20-day MA crosses above 50-day MA - indicates strengthening upside momentum.

Bearish crossover when 20-day MA drops below 50-

day MA - flags potential emerging downtrend.

Oscillators like RSI aid timing of entries. For e.g. buy when RSI crosses above 50.

## Sensex Technical Analysis

Sensex comprises 30 well established and financially sound large cap stocks representing various sectors of the economy.

Sensex exhibits similar technical patterns as Nifty - ranging phases, breakouts, pullbacks, swing moves, moving average crosses.

Analysis techniques remain broadly similar - identify bias directionally using 20, 50, 200 day MAs. Buy pullbacks and dips in uptrends. Look to short rallies in downtrends. Play within trading ranges by buying low and selling high.

However, Sensex tends to be less volatile compared to Nifty due to index composition. Reversals from extremes often less pronounced on Sensex. Thus verify indications on Nifty before applying signals on Sensex.

- **Stock Trading Examples**

Now let's see examples of trading techniques applied on individual stocks:

## Infosys

Move above Rs 800 in May 2020 marked upside breakout from long consolidation indicating bull trend start.

RSI moving above 50 in April 2020 signaled positive momentum building up.

20-day MA consistently provided support on dips during uptrend.

## Reliance

Double bottom pattern with positive divergence on RSI in March 2020 pointed to trend reversal up.

MACD line crossing above signal line generated further buy signal.

Break above Rs 1,400 and previous high confirmed upside breakout.

## TCS

Downtrend from Jan 2022 high made lower highs and lows. 20-day MA provided resistance.

RSI divergence at Sept 2022 low signalled upside momentum revival.

Break above intermediate resistance at Rs 3,400 flagged bullish trend reversal.

## HDFC Bank

Bull flag continuation pattern in June 2021 provided low risk entry. Target of Rs 1,800 achieved.

Daily upper Bollinger band capped advances repeatedly between Sept-Dec 2021 highlighting potential topping formation.

Thus combining indicators, patterns and techniques described earlier can produce effective trading system rules. Practice is key to refine strategies further. Please feel free to suggest any specific examples or trading strategies I could elaborate on with charts. Look forward to your inputs.

# Chapter 4 - Value Investing

## 4.1 Introduction

Value investing involves identifying and investing in stocks trading at prices significantly below their intrinsic values. It relies on fundamental analysis to discover high quality but temporarily beaten down businesses available at attractive valuations. The strategy was pioneered and popularized by Benjamin Graham and David Dodd through seminal books like Security Analysis and The Intelligent Investor.

Graham introduced key concepts like margin of safety, Mr. Market metaphor and emphasis on quantifiable factors. Value investors only buy when the market price offers a discount to conservative estimates of intrinsic value which acts as the margin of safety. This principle helps limit downside. Valuations are assessed using metrics like P/E, P/B ratios, earnings yield and asset value. Discounted cash flow models determine projected value based on long term earnings power and fundamentals.

The Mr. Market metaphor views the overall market as a moody business partner who offers to sell or buy out the investor at varying prices each day. The disciplined investor aims to take advantage of the volatility in Mr. Market's emotions by buying assets from him at low prices and selling when he overpays, rather than be influenced by greed or fear. Fundamental analysis skills help value investors determine when market mispricing occurs relative to intrinsic value.

Warren Buffett and Charlie Munger further expanded value investing philosophy with concepts like economic moats, margin of safety, circles of competence, and retaining earnings to compound growth. High quality, easy to understand businesses with durable competitive advantages, consistent earnings power, solid management and low capital needs are favored. Growth is viewed as a component of value. Superior long term returns rely on investing in such compounding machines.

Patience is critical as undervalued situations often take time to realize full value. Tracking quarterly results helps assess business trajectory. Portfolio concentration in best ideas boosts outperformance but also increases volatility. Exit discipline gets enforced when prices exceed intrinsic value significantly.

Academic evidence offers strong support for value investing strategies outperforming broader markets across long horizons of 10-15 years given the contrarian nature of buying during low valuations. However, the strategy enjoys less consistent outperformance over shorter periods. Market exuberance can prolong overvaluation of growth stocks. Tracking earnings helps gauge when market realizes mispricing.

In dynamic Indian markets, value investors need to be watchful of management quality, leverage risk, disruptions, accounting quality and volatility risk concentrated portfolios face. Competitive advantages are also transient as new players rapidly gain share. But the focus on margin of safety makes value investing well suited for Indian markets despite higher volatility. Calibrating to Indian context can aid success.

The advent of digitalization, big data and computing power has made screening tools and databases easily accessible for finding undervalued opportunities. But human oversight and discretion remains essential.

Patience and discipline are integral as ever to holding through volatility until intrinsic value gets realized. In summary, value investing remains a robust strategy if implemented prudently adhering to core principles. In the forthcoming sections, we will explore nuances, tools, case studies and contemporary context for successful value investing.

$$\vdash \Omega\,\Omega\,\Omega\,\Omega\,\Omega\,\Omega\,\Omega\,\Omega\,\Omega\,\Omega\,\Omega\,\Omega\,\Omega\,\Omega\,\Omega\,\Omega\,\Omega\,\Omega\,\Omega\,\Omega\,\Omega \dashv$$

## 4.2 Warren Buffett's Core Principles

Warren Buffett is widely regarded as the greatest value investor of our times. His strong track record of generating 20%+ compounded annual returns for six decades makes him the ideal role model. By analyzing Buffett's approach and philosophy, we can gain deep insights into successful value investing.

### Focus on Long Term Compounding

Buffett's goal is to generate consistent long term growth in per-share intrinsic value which gets reflected in stock price over time. He focuses on identifying businesses with sustainable competitive advantages that support durable earnings growth to compound capital.

Rather than aim for quick speculative gains or try timing markets, Buffett remains focused on long-term horizon and lets the power of compounding work. Patience is integral to allow fundamentals and growth to drive returns over full market cycles.

## High Quality Businesses

Buffett seeks businesses with strong fundamentals - proven track record, strong competitive advantages (or "economic moats"), capable management, robust financial health and good growth prospects.

He prefers relatively simple to understand businesses versus complex structures or rapid changes. Simple predictable business models with clarity on drivers lends confidence in estimates and projections.

Good management is critical as leadership shapes strategy and capital allocation. Buffett evaluates managers for high integrity, passion, talent retention and rational capital deployment.

## Margin of Safety

The difference between intrinsic value and market price is the "margin of safety". This buffer protects from misjudgements or unexpected events.

Buffett wants a discount of at least 30% to estimated intrinsic value before investing. The wider the gap, the higher the returns and lower the risk.

Conservative assumptions for growth and valuations establish margin of safety. Favorable upside surprises can boost returns.

## Long Term View on Risk

Rather than view portfolio volatility as risk, Buffett sees risk as potential for permanent capital loss. He mitigates this risk by not overpaying relative to intrinsic value.

Buffett's acceptance of price volatility allows him to maximize long term returns by exploiting fear and greed driven mispricing. Avoiding leverage also reduces volatility risk.

Focus on earnings power over market sentiment provides resilience. However, risks still need prudent assessment.

## Focus on Value, Not Price

Buffett focuses on identifying divergence between market price and intrinsic value. Stock price frequently digresses from business value but ultimately converges over long term.

Rather than attempt market timing, he waits patiently for sound investments at attractive prices instead of chasing overpriced stocks.

Quantifying value and comparing to prevailing prices reveals the margin of safety to buffer against downside.

Now let's examine a real example analyzing Apple using Buffett's lens:

## Apple Case Study

Competitive Advantage - Apple has strong brand loyalty, premium pricing power and ecosystem lock-in effect that gives its wide economic moat. Brand value, successful innovation pipeline and high switching costs confer durable edge.

Financial Health - Very strong balance sheet with $54 billion cash, $115 billion debt. Profitability is robust with 45% gross margins and 26% net profit margins. High ROE of 147%. Good liquidity and working capital.

Management - Visionary leadership and excellent execution track record by Tim Cook since taking over in 2011. Strong bench strength and succession planning.

Growth Runway - Installed base of 1.8 billion devices provides foundation for services growth. Wearables, health and subscription revenues will expand domain beyond hardware. Strong brand allows pricing power.

Valuation - Apple trades at P/E of 27 based on FY22 EPS of $6. At conservative 10-15% growth, fair value works out to $240. Trading at ~10% discount provides margin of safety.

In summary, Buffett's value investing core tenets of longevity, quality, growth, proven management and margin of safety are strongly applicable while assessing Apple. The business fundamentals stack up compellingly and downside appears cushioned.

## Circle of Competence

Buffett stresses staying within one's circle of competence where the investor has knowledge and expertise when analysing companies. Venturing outside domains of experience can be risky.

For example, there are businesses like advanced technology or biotech which require specific skills and deeper industry insight to evaluate properly.Without competence, analysis can go wrong.

Buffett understands consumer brands, insurance and industrials well given decades of exposure. This allows him to develop robust insights. Investors should play to their strengths.

## Sit On Hands And Wait

"The stock market is designed to transfer money from the active to the patient."

Buffett is willing to hold large cash balances for extended periods while waiting for fat pitch undervalued opportunities.

Rather than remain fully invested regardless of valuations, he bides his time for the right opportunities. This hands-off approach minimizes mistakes.

Patience combined with decisiveness when high conviction opportunity arises elevates success probability.

## Model of Investing Greats

Buffett has referred to Ben Graham's book The Intelligent Investor as the best book ever on investing. He considers Graham his mentor and guru.

He has also highlighted Phil Fisher's book Common Stocks and Uncommon Profits which promoted scuttlebutt research going beyond just numbers.

Studying proven investment philosophies helps develop robust mental frameworks and thought processes.

## 20-Punch Card Test

"If you gave me a punch card with only twenty punches, and each represented a lifetime investment choice, I'd want to make those choices very carefully."

This analogy indicates Buffett's focused approach - make a few high conviction long term investments instead of frequent trading.

Concentrating capital in best ideas after thorough analysis rather than over-diversify helps generate outsized returns. Conviction and discipline are key.

## Mr. Market Metaphor

Mr. Market represents the overall market mood which swings between fear and greed, driving prices way above and below intrinsic value.

Buffett exploits this market folly by acting as a rational long term business owner, buying undervalued assets from Mr. Market when he sells cheap.

Independent thinking inoculates against market sentiment. Objective study of business fundamentals anchors decisions.

By following Buffett's timeless tenets explained above, long term investors can master the art of value investing with patience and discipline. I hope these examples give you a good overview of implementing

Buffett's principles.

⊢ Ω Ω Ω Ω Ω Ω Ω Ω Ω Ω Ω Ω Ω Ω Ω Ω Ω Ω Ω Ω Ω Ω Ω ⊣

## 4.3 Margin of Safety and Circle of Competence

Margin of safety and circle of competence are interrelated value investing principles emphasized by Warren Buffett. Let's examine them in detail with examples:

### Margin of Safety

Margin of safety means purchasing stocks at a significant discount to their estimated intrinsic or fundamental value. This provides downside protection in case the analysis is flawed or unexpected risks emerge. The concept was stressed in Ben Graham's teachings as well.

### Steps to ensure margin of safety:

- Estimate intrinsic value conservatively using proven valuation models like discounted cash flow, relative valuations, asset-based models etc.
- Demand a discount of at least 30% to intrinsic value before considering investment. The wider probability-weighted.
- Use conservative assumptions for projections. Do not rely on best-case scenarios playing out.
- Assess downside risks and probability-weighted scenarios. Avoid companies with high uncertainty or leverage.
- Have long investment horizon of 5+ years for value to realize. Be prepared to hold through volatility.

- Diversify prudently to avoid concentration risk. But don't over-diversify just for sake of dilution.
- Keep sufficient cash reserves to exploit market declines presenting bargains. Don't remain fully invested.

**Benefits of margin of safety:**

- Downside protection if projections not met.
- Improved upside potential given undervaluation.
- Ability to weather short term volatility.
- Higher confidence in investment thesis.
- Forces discipline in security selection. Avoid speculative stories.

The margin of safety also grows as the company executes well and price remains stagnant. This offers opportunity to allocate more capital into the high conviction idea at an even better price later.

Let's take the example of Asian Paints to assess margin of safety:

## Asian Paints

- Leading decorative paints franchise with strong brand equity. 54% market share in India.
- Financials very healthy - debt free, 40% return on equity, 25% EBITDA margins.
- Valuation - Trading at P/E of 80x and P/B of 20x. Earnings have grown at 13% CAGR over 5 years.
- Intrinsic value estimated at Rs 3,000 based on relative valuation of 60x PE on forward earnings.
- Current market price is Rs 3,100. Limited margin of safety with only 3% downside buffer.

Margin of safety would improve significantly if purchased at corrections to Rs 2,500 for example.

Thus, currently Asian Paints doesn't present an adequate margin of safety despite leadership position given the high absolute valuation. Investors need to wait patiently for better entry point to improve odds of strong returns.

## **Circle of Competence**

This refers to the sphere of knowledge and expertise of the investor. Assessing companies beyond one's circle of competence increases the risk of flawed assumptions or judgement errors.

Ways to remain in the circle of competence:

- Invest in sectors where you have professional experience like technology, banking etc.
- Avoid complex or opaque businesses. Favor simple transparent business models.
- Track specific industries for years to develop sound understanding before investing.
- Study thoroughly to expand your competence circle gradually into new domains.
- Seek experts' opinions to fill knowledge gaps while doing own due diligence.
- Maintain checklist of key questions and factors specific to sector/industry to guide analysis.

## **Common beginner errors:**

- Investing in "hot themes" without deeper understanding. E.g. cryptocurrencies, NFTs.
- Getting swayed by narratives or projections by

external experts without internalizing.

- Relying on general intuition rather than concrete metrics or industry insights.
- Anchoring biases and blind spots are common when assessing businesses beyond core competence.

While competence gaps can be bridged through practice over time, it is prudent to recognize one's circle of competence and stay within it when starting out. Let's take an example:

## Metals Sector

Complex interplay of demand-supply metrics, commodity cycles, forex movements.
High capital intensity. Challenging cost economics with volatile raw material input prices.
Requires deeper understanding of mining, smelting, inventory management etc.
Best avoided by investors without direct experience given higher complexity and opacity.
In summary, circle of competence enables focus on sound opportunities while margin of safety helps protect downside when investing within that circle. The two concepts offer synergistic advantages in risk management.

⊢ΩΩΩΩΩΩΩΩΩΩΩΩΩΩΩΩΩΩΩΩΩΩ⊣

## 4.4 Valuation Models

Valuation models form the crux of determining intrinsic value in value investing. By applying various valuation techniques, investors estimate the fair value range of a business. The two most popular approaches are discounted cash flow (DCF) analysis and relative valuation using comparable multiples.

## **Discounted Cash Flow Analysis**

DCF analysis involves forecasting future free cash flows from the business and discounting them back to the present using the weighted average cost of capital to derive a net present value.

## **Steps:**

1) Project free cash flows (FCF) for the next 5-10 years based on revenue growth rates, operating margins, capex, depreciation, working capital assumptions etc.
2) Estimate terminal value beyond the explicit forecast period using stable growth rate.
3) Determine appropriate discount rate or WACC based on cost of equity and cost of debt based on comparable.
4) Discount each year's FCF and terminal value to the present.
5) Sum up discounted values to get net present value which is the DCF valuation.

## **DCF advantages:**

- Directly based on business fundamentals and cash generation potential.
- Flexibility to model different growth scenarios and sensitivities.
- Captures full value of growth companies.
- Suitable for stable, predictable businesses.

## **DCF limitations:**

- Requires making projections into the future which inherently involves uncertainty.
- Small changes in WACC or growth rates can materially impact valuation.
- Does not fully capture competitive dynamics and risks.
- More suitable for mature companies than earlier stage high growth firms.

Let's take the example of performing DCF analysis on **TCS:**

## TCS DCF Model

- Revenue CAGR forecast at 13% for next 5 years and 6% terminal growth rate based on historical trends and industry outlook.
- Operating profit margin expected to remain stable at 25%. Conservative EBIT margin of 22% used for projections.
- Depreciation and capex projections based on historic levels scaled up for growth. Non-cash charges adjusted.
- Working capital assumptions include 2 months receivables, 1 month payables cycle.
- Cost of equity taken as 14% based on comparable mature IT services firms.
- Cost of debt observed as 7.5%. 72% equity, 28% debt weights used to derive WACC of 12%.
- On discounting FCFs at 12% WACC, intrinsic value arrives at Rs. 3400 per share.
- Provides adequate 31% margin of safety over market price of Rs 2600.

Thus DCF helps establish valuation range based on

business fundamentals. Sensitivity analysis on key assumptions is advised.

## Relative Valuation

Relative valuation is based on comparing valuation ratios like P/E, EV/EBITDA, P/B of the company being valued versus ratios of comparable listed firms in the same industry.

### Approach:

1) Identify listed peers with similar business model, markets, scale. Around 5-6 comparables preferred.
2) Calculate current valuation ratios like forward P/E, P/B, EV/Revenue, EV/EBITDA for comparables. Determine mean or median.
3) Compare company's ratios versus peers to see if it is undervalued, overvalued or fairly priced.
4) If undervalued, estimate fair value based on adjusting ratios closer to peer averages.

**Pros of relative valuation:**

- Simpler compared to DCF. Easily understandable.
- Directly reveals if company is richly or cheaply valued relatively.
- Accounts for current market sentiment towards sector.

**Cons:**

- Difficult to find perfectly comparable companies differing only in valuation.
- Very sensitive to choice of right peer group.

Wrong peer group can skew estimates.
- Does not fully consider company's growth outlook, risks, competitive position.
- Works better for companies later in life-cycle.

## HDFC Bank Relative Valuation

- Peers - Kotak Bank, ICICI Bank, Axis Bank, SBI
- HDFC Bank trades at 4x P/B and 18x P/E based on FY22 EPS of Rs 68
- Peers average P/B is 3x and P/E is 16x
- Assigning 15x P/E multiple yields fair value estimate of Rs 1000
- 23% upside suggests HDFC Bank offers attractive risk-reward

In summary, prudent use of both DCF and relative valuation models offers a comprehensive framework for determining intrinsic value. Blending both techniques along with qualitative assessment compensates for individual limitations.

⊢ΩΩΩΩΩΩΩΩΩΩΩΩΩΩΩΩΩΩΩΩΩΩ⊣

## 4.5 Case Studies of Leading Value Investors in India

By examining the investing frameworks and stock selection principles used by India's most successful value investors, we can gain valuable insights into their thought process and approach. Let's take a look at 4 leading value investors:

### Rakesh Jhunjhunwala

- Known as India's Warren Buffett with net worth of over \$6 billion. Generated CAGR of ~25% since 1985.
- Core philosophy - identify and bet big on India's structural growth story across sectors like banking, infrastructure, FMCG, pharma etc.
- Focused portfolio of 15-20 stocks primarily midcap opportunities. Aims for multibagger return over 3-5 years.
- Conducts rigorous bottom up research. Assesses management pedigree and corporate governance practices closely.
- Known for investing based on macroeconomic analysis and identifying inflection points in business cycle like uptrend in private capex.
- Bullish on banks with low NPA and niche focus. Bet big on private sector banks prior to 2008 boom period.
- Key successes - Titan, Lupin, Crisil. Exited huge winners like Infosys, IPCA Labs early.

## **Prashant Jain**

- CIO of HDFC Mutual Fund. Grown assets under management from ₹3,000 crore to over ₹4 lakh crore. Delivered 19% CAGR since 2003.
- Investing style - buy high quality names during phases of irrational pessimism. Ride momentum uptrends.
- Diversified portfolio spanning 50-80 stocks across market caps and sectors. High churn ratio.
- Exits when valuations become excessive relative to fundamentals. Known for cash calls at market peaks.
- Leverages fund house research capabilities to

identify emerging sectors and themes early like corporate banks, pharma, consumer trends etc.
- Key successes - HDFC Bank, Bajaj Finance, Page Industries, Gruh Finance.

## Saurabh Mukherjea

- Founder of Marcellus Investment Managers. $1.5 billion AUM. Focused long-only public equities fund.
- Investment principles - consistency, governance, scalability. Build concentrated portfolio of 10-15 high quality names.
- Rigorous due diligence into 5 categories - size, longevity, business model, financial parameters, management quality.
- Buys companies with consistent growth, high RoCE, low debt. Sells when valuations exceed fair value or fundamentals deteriorate.
- Essential reading is his book "The Unusual Billionaires". Cuts through market noise and focuses on business fundamentals.
- Key successes - Page Industries, HDFC Bank, Kotak Bank, Bajaj Finance.

## Rajeev Thakkar

- CIO of PPFAS Mutual Fund managing flagship Parag Parikh Flexi Cap Fund. Delivered 17% CAGR since inception in 2013.
- Core tenets - right price, growth orientation, management quality, low leverage, valuations relative to earnings growth.
- Concentrated portfolio of 25-30 high conviction stocks spanning market caps and sectors.
- Willing to pay premium for visible growth but

only up to a reasonable limit. Exits when valuations become excessive.
- High active share of over 80% reflecting truly active stock picking rather than benchmark hugging.
- Key successes - Page Industries, HDFC Bank, Marico. Underweight in expensive stocks like ITC, HUL.

In summary, maintaining a concentrated portfolio of quality businesses bought at reasonable valuations and a willingness to take cash calls emerge as common success traits among leading value investors in India. Developing a solid analytical foundation and patience helps capitalize when risks get mispriced by the market. I hope these real world illustrations offer useful perspectives into implementing value investing effectively.

# Chapter 5 – Options Trading

## 5.1 Introduction

Options are financial derivatives based on an underlying asset which can be stocks, indices, commodities, currencies etc. Options give buyers the right but not the obligation to buy or sell the underlying asset at the strike price on or before the expiration date. Sellers of options take on the obligation to fulfill the transaction if the buyer exercises the option.

Call options give the buyer the right to buy the underlying asset while put options give the right to sell. Options were introduced in India in 2001 and are traded on the NSE, BSE and MCX exchanges. They provide powerful financial tools for hedging, speculating and income generation strategies due to inherent leverage advantage.

Options pricing factors include current spot price of underlying, strike price which is the fixed price agreed, expiration date till which option can be exercised, volatility which indicates price fluctuations and time remaining to expiry which impacts time value. Premium is the upfront amount paid by option buyer to the seller. Options can expire worthless if spot price is unfavorable to the strike price on expiry.

Open interest denotes the total number of outstanding option contracts held by market participants for a given strike price and expiry date. Higher open interest indicates stronger commitment and liquidity. Options offer asymmetric payoff as the buyer's loss is limited to the premium paid while gains have uncapped upside if the underlying moves favorably. Sellers face uncapped losses if the spot moves against their position.

Moneyness indicates the relationship between spot and strike price. Options trading deep in the money when spot is significantly above strike for calls and below strike for puts have high intrinsic value and less time value. At the money options when spot equals strike price only have time value equal to the premium. Out-of-the-money options have zero intrinsic value only time value and are riskiest to hold.

Option profitability is measured using the Greeks - Delta indicates option price change per Rs. 1 change in underlying spot. Gamma indicates an acceleration in Delta. Theta denotes time decay in extrinsic value each day. Vega indicates sensitivity to volatility.

Options trading strategies allow expressing market views directionally like bullish, bearish or neutral outlooks. Strategies involve combining options with differing strike prices, underlying assets and expiry schedules to structure a desired payoff graph. Common strategies include long calls and puts, covered calls, bull and bear spreads, straddles, strangles etc.

Successful options traders develop a sound understanding of market conditions using technical and volatility analysis. They apply strategies with an edge like selling overpriced options, playing mean reversion in volatility, leveraging mispricings between correlated assets etc. Risk management is critical given leverage. In the forthcoming chapters, we will explore options concepts, payoff graphs, Greek parameters and effective trading strategies in detail.

⊢ Ω Ω Ω Ω Ω Ω Ω Ω Ω Ω Ω Ω Ω Ω Ω Ω Ω Ω Ω Ω Ω Ω Ω ⊣

## 5.2 Options Theory and Concepts

Options are financial instruments that give buyers the right, but not the obligation, to buy or sell an underlying asset at a pre-determined strike price on or before the expiration date. The underlying asset can be stocks, indices, commodities, currencies etc. Let's examine the fundamental concepts of options theory:

## **Call Options**

A call option gives the holder the right to buy the underlying asset at the strike price on or before the expiry date.

For example, an Infosys 1640 call option gives the buyer the right to purchase Infosys shares at Rs. 1,640 on or before the expiry date.

The buyer pays an upfront premium to the seller/writer for this right. If Infosys is trading above 1640 on expiry, the call buyer can exercise the option and earn the difference. Else the option expires worthless.

## **Put Options**

A put option gives the holder the right to sell the underlying at the strike price on or before expiry.

For example, an RIL 2480 put option gives the buyer the right to sell Reliance shares at Rs. 2480 on or before expiry.

If Reliance is trading below 2480 on expiry, the put buyer can exercise the option and earn the difference between 2480 and lower spot price. Else this put option too expires worthless.

## Strike Price

The strike price, also called exercise price, is the fixed price at which the option buyer can buy or sell the underlying asset if the option is exercised.

It is a standardized price set by the exchange. For example 25000 strike call and put options on Nifty index.

## Premium

The premium is the upfront amount paid by the options buyer to the seller to purchase the option. Premium compensates the seller for the risk undertaken.

Higher premiums imply higher pricing of underlying volatility. Premium depends on factors like underlying price, strike price, time to expiry and volatility.

## Expiration Date

The expiration date or expiry is the last date on which the options contract is valid. Expiry is always on the 3rd Thursday of the expiry month.

For example, October 2022 expiry will be on 20th October which is 3rd Thursday. On expiry, option either gets exercised or expires worthless.

## Open Interest

Open interest is the total number of outstanding option contracts held by market participants for a given strike price and expiry.

Higher open interest indicates greater liquidity and trader participation to close positions. Options with low open interest are usually avoided.

## In the Money (ITM)

If spot price is above strike price for call options or below strike for put options, the option is said to be in the money. Such options have intrinsic value in addition to time value.

For example, 1500 strike calls are ITM when Infosys is at 1600. 2500 puts are ITM when Reliance is at 2400.

## Out of the Money (OTM)

When spot is below strike for calls or above strike for puts, the option has no intrinsic value and only time value remaining. Such options are out of the money.

For instance, 1800 calls are OTM if Infosys is at 1600. 2400 puts are OTM if Reliance is at 2500.

## At the Money (ATM)

When spot equals strike price, the option is at the money. It carries only time value equal to the premium and no intrinsic value.

For example, if Bank Nifty index is at 41000, 41000 strike calls and puts are at the money.

## **Moneyness**

Moneyness indicates the relationship between the option strike price and underlying spot price. It determines whether the option has intrinsic value or only time value based on being ITM, ATM or OTM.

In summary, these key parameters determine options pricing, payoffs, profitability and trading strategies. A strong grasp of options theory provides a robust foundation for effective trading. We will next look at options payoffs, profit calculations and Greek parameters.

$$\vdash \Omega\,\Omega\,\Omega\,\Omega\,\Omega\,\Omega\,\Omega\,\Omega\,\Omega\,\Omega\,\Omega\,\Omega\,\Omega\,\Omega\,\Omega\,\Omega\,\Omega\,\Omega\,\Omega\,\Omega\,\Omega\,\Omega\,\Omega\,\Omega \dashv$$

## 5.3 Options Greeks

Options Greeks measure the sensitivity of option premiums to various risk parameters. By understanding Greeks, traders can estimate the change in premiums related to movements in underlying price, volatility, time decay etc. Mastery over Greeks allows creating options positions with desired risk-reward payoff.

The 4 major Greeks are **Delta**, **Gamma**, **Theta** and **Vega**. We will also discuss **Rho** and **Omega**.

## **Delta**

- Delta indicates the degree and direction of change in option premium corresponding to a 1 unit change in the underlying asset price.

- Call option Delta ranges between 0 to 1. Higher

the Delta, more the premium rises when underlying price increases.

- Put option Delta ranges between -1 to 0. More negative Delta indicates premium rising as underlying price declines.
- ITM options have higher Delta closer to 1 or -1 based on higher intrinsic value.
- OTM options have lower Delta tending towards 0 as only time value remains.

## Gamma

Gamma measures rate of change in Delta itself for small movements in underlying price. Higher Gamma implies Delta changing more rapidly.

Gamma is highest when option is at the money as time value erodes fastest nearing expiry.
Gamma indicates the acceleration in rate of change of premium value. Helpful to adjust positions rapidly.

## Theta

Theta indicates the time decay in option premium each day as expiry approaches due to erosion in extrinsic time value.

Time value decays faster in last 30 days as optionality decreases nearing expiry.

Theta is highest for ATM options as entire premium equals time value. OTM options have lower Theta.
Negative Theta indicates losing value due to time decay each day. Positive Theta means gaining premium with passing time.

## Vega

Vega measures sensitivity in option value to changes in volatility of the underlying asset. Higher Vega means premium rising more with volatility.

- Vega is high when option is ATM as time value has maximum sensitivity to volatility.
- Vega declines as option goes deep ITM or OTM. Also falls nearing expiry.
- Compare Vega when choosing between contracts expiring in 30 days vs 60 days.

## Rho

Rho indicates sensitivity of option value to changes in risk free interest rate. Higher Rho means higher rate sensitivity.

Typically, low impact since interest rate moves are usually small.
More relevant for longer duration options like LEAPs.

## Omega

Omega measures sensitivity in option's Gamma to changes in underlying price. It indicates rate of change in Gamma.

Used to gauge how fast Gamma erodes, especially when option goes deep ITM or OTM.

Enables adjustments to leveraged positions where Gamma scalping is employed.

Now let's examine a practical example to demonstrate application of Greeks:

## **Infosys 1640 Call Example**

- Infosys spot price: Rs 1600
- Strike price of call option: Rs 1640
- Days remaining: 45
- Volatility: 25%
- Interest rate: 5%
- Premium: Rs 40
- Delta: 0.5
- Gamma: 0.06
- Theta: -2.5
- Vega: 30

### **Interpretation:**

- Rs 1 rise in Infosys spot can result in Rs 0.5 rise in premium due to Delta of 0.5
- Gamma of 0.06 means Delta change accelerates by 0.06 per Rs 1 change in underlying.
- Theta -2.5 indicates daily time decay of Rs 2.5 in premium with passing day.
- Vega 30 signals Rs 30 rise in premium if volatility rises 1%

In summary, Greeks allow anticipating the risk-reward payoff dynamically and managing positions accordingly. Mastery over Greeks elevates trading strategies significantly.

⊢ΩΩΩΩΩΩΩΩΩΩΩΩΩΩΩΩΩΩΩΩΩΩ⊣

## **5.4 Options Trading Strategies**

Options offer a versatile toolkit allowing traders to

express directional market views, generate income, hedge positions and structure varied risk-reward payoffs through combinations. Let's explore the major strategies:

## Long Calls

Buying call options to benefit from an upside move in the underlying asset. Pays off when spot rises above strike price by more than the premium paid.

Benefits from unlimited upside if strong rally happens. Loss limited to premium paid if rally doesn't materialize.
Choose strike at or slightly above technical resistance where breakout is expected.
Exit on rally to target or if support breaks implying downtrend.

## Long Puts

Buying put options to profit from expected down move. Pays off if spot declines below strike price by more than put premium.

Enables benefiting from sharp falls while capping maximum loss to premium paid.
Select strike at or slightly below support where breakdown expected.
Exit on drop to target or if resistance breaks signaling upside.

## Covered Calls

Holding underlying asset and simultaneously selling call options against it. Call premium earned provides income.

1. If spot is below strike on expiry, enjoy premium as income. If call exercises, exit asset at favorable strike price.
2. Select strike at resistance where unwilling to sell asset below price.
3. Exit option position to capture further upside if strong breakout above strike.

## Married Puts

Holding asset and simultaneously buying protective put options. Puts hedge downside risk.

1. Puts kick in protection if asset price falls below strike. Upside remains unlimited.
2. Choose strike well below strong support to define downside buffer.
3. Exit put to retain all upside if resistance breaks on volumes.

## Bull Call Spread

Buying lower strike calls and simultaneously selling same expiry higher strike calls. Limits premium outflow.

Maximum profit if spot closes above higher strike on expiry. Loss capped at net premium paid.
Helps reduce premium outflow compared to outright call buying.

## Bear Put Spread

Buying higher strike puts while simultaneously selling

lower strike puts to fund some of the purchase.

Max profit if spot closes below lower strike on expiry.
Loss limited to net premium paid.
Lowers net premium outflow compared to outright put buying.

## Straddle

Buying both ATM call and put of same strike and expiry. Benefits from high volatility in either direction.

Profits if sharp move above or below strike by more than combined premiums paid. Else loss.

Performs when there is uncertainty regarding direction but expecting volatility expansion ahead.

## Strangle

Buying OTM call and put instead of ATM options. Cheaper premium than straddle.

Pays off if spot moves sharply beyond OTM strike prices by more than premiums paid.

More room for underlying to make big move since OTM strikes chosen.

## Butterfly Spread

Involves combining call and put options strategically at adjacent strike prices to create a payoff resembling a butterfly shape.

Combines bull spread and bear spread.

Low cost strategy. Profits from time decay if spot is rangebound. Loses in sharp uptrend/downtrend.

## Risk Reversal

Combines simultaneous buying of OTM call and selling of OTM put with same expiry. Market neutral.

Constructed to have zero net premium cost through appropriate strike selection.
Profits from uptick in volatility. Requires low directional bias.

## Ratio Spread

Involves uneven number of options bought versus sold at different strike prices to skew risk-reward.

For example - buying 2 ITM calls and selling 1 OTM call of same expiry.

skews payoff favorably, enabling bigger gains if view is very bullish.
Tailored for specific market outlook by configuring risk-reward payoff.

In summary, strategies offer varied payoffs - directional, volatility, skewed, income etc. Combined prudently and traded with discipline, options enable participating across diverse market conditions.

## Iron Condor

The iron condor combines a bull put spread and a

bear call spread. It aims to profit from rangebound sideways movement in the underlying.

## Construction:

Sell out of the money put and another higher strike out of the money call to collect premiums

Buy further out of the money put and call to define risk if extreme move happens

## Ideal scenario:

- Underlying trades in a tight range such that sold puts and calls expire worthless allowing to retain premium received

- Loss risk is defined on downside by lower put strike and upside by higher call strike

- Works well when expecting low volatility contraction ahead and neutral outlook. Requires active adjustment to prevent unlimited loss on breakout.

## Jade Lizard

The jade lizard strategy combines a bull call vertical spread with a sold out of the money put. Allows upside participation with downside protection.

## Construction:

Sell out of the money put to collect premium
Buy lower strike call and sell higher strike call to form bull call spread

## Ideal scenario:

- If underlying rallies, gains from the bull call spread. OTM put expires worthless.
- If underlying declines moderately, keep premium from sold put to cushion downside. Call spread expires worthless.
- Sold put strike defines maximum loss if there is sharp fall below that level.
- Appropriate when moderately bullish to benefit from upside while also collecting time premium. Requires adjustment on heavy sell off.

## Diagonal Spread

This strategy combines options of differing strike prices and expiration dates. Adds additional dimension.

## Construction:

Buy longer dated call option for directional exposure
Sell shorter dated call at higher strike to fund long call and collect time premium

## Ideal scenario:

- If rally happens quickly within near term expiration, capture gains from short call
- If ascent happens later, gains from lower strike longer
- dated call.
- Short call limits loss in sideways or downward move scenarios
- Works well when expecting rally but unsure of

precise timing. Requires actively rolling short call position to maximize gains.

Now let's examine some trading examples on index options:

## Iron Condor on Nifty

- Nifty trading between 17200 and 17400 in consolidating range
- Sold 17400 call for Rs 100 premium and bought 17700 call for Rs 25 to limit upside risk
- Sold 16800 put for Rs 150 premium and bought 16500 put for Rs 50 to define downside risk
- Range play results in profit of Rs 175 through expiry if Nifty stays between short strikes

## Jade Lizard on Bank Nifty

- Moderately bullish on Bank Nifty trading at 42000
- Sold 43500 put at Rs 100 premium for downside buffer
- Bought 42100 call for Rs 250 and sold 42400 call for Rs 150 constructing bull call spread

## Diagonal Call Spread on Reliance

- Bullish on Reliance but unsure if rally will happen soon
- Bought 3 month 2400 call for Rs 250
- Sold 1 month 2550 call for Rs 100 to lower net cost

Thus combining options vertically across strikes and

horizontally across expiries allows crafting strategies aligned with market outlook. Over time, traders gain intuition for visualizing payoff graphs and scenario analysis.

$$\vdash \Omega\,\Omega\,\Omega\,\Omega\,\Omega\,\Omega\,\Omega\,\Omega\,\Omega\,\Omega\,\Omega\,\Omega\,\Omega\,\Omega\,\Omega\,\Omega\,\Omega\,\Omega\,\Omega\,\Omega\,\Omega\,\Omega\,\Omega\,\Omega \dashv$$

## 5.5 Options Trading Examples

By examining options trading examples across indices and stocks, we can better understand how traders apply principles in practice to profit across diverse market conditions. Let's discuss 20 examples:

### Nifty Put Calendar Spread

- Market outlook: Bearish near term, neutral longer term

- Strategy: Sell current month 19000 put for Rs 150, Buy next month 19000 put for Rs 250

- Created put calendar spread to benefit from expected drop in Nifty in current expiry while giving time for rebound later. Captured short term volatility skew.

### Bank Nifty Call Diagonal

- Market outlook: Bullish bias, unsure of timing

- Strategy: Buy 3 month 44000 call for Rs 600, Sell 1 month 44800 call for Rs 300

- Constructed call diagonal to gain long directional exposure while funding part of premium via short dated OTM call sale.

## Reliance Bear Put Spread

- Market outlook: Moderately bearish expecting limited downside

- Strategy: Buy 2400 put for Rs 120, Sell 2200 put for Rs 70

- Put spread limits loss if decline is gradual while benefiting from sharp fall below 2200. Capped risk to Rs 50 net premium paid.

## Infosys Long Straddle

- Market outlook: Volatility expansion expected

- Strategy: Buy 1600 strike call for Rs 75, 1600 strike put for Rs 60 ahead of results

- Long straddle to benefit from expected volatility expansion on either side due to results. Maximum loss limited to Rs 135 premium paid if flat.

## HDFC Bank Short Strangle

- Market outlook: Rangebound movement expected

- Strategy: Sold 1400 call for Rs 35, 1400 put for Rs 50. Collected net premium of Rs 85.

- Short strangle capitalizes on expected low volatility. Pocket premium if HDFC Bank trades between strikes on expiry. Uncapped loss beyond strikes.

## Kotak Bank Call Ratio Spread

- Market outlook: Very bullish on strong results

- Strategy: Buy 2 lots 1900 call for Rs 300, Sell 1 lot 2000 call for 200

- Bought more lower strike calls than higher strike to skew payoff favorably for big rally post results. Net cost reduced while retaining upside exposure.

## ITC Long Call Butterfly

- Market outlook: Rangebound with mild bullish bias

- Strategy: Buy 240 call for Rs 12, Sell 2 265 calls for Rs 6 each, Buy 275 call for Rs 3. Net cost Rs 3.

- Constructed long call butterfly for low debit. Maximum profit between middle short strikes if ITC trades rangebound. Uncapped loss in sharp rallies/declines.

## Axis Bank Bear Call Ladder

- Market outlook: Moderately bearish expecting

gradual descent

- Strategy: Sold 850 call for Rs 20, Sold 800 call for Rs 40, Bought 750 call for Rs 60

- Ladder with incremental short call strikes to benefit from gradual decline. Collected net premium. Uncapped loss below 750.

## SBI Short Call Calendar

- Market Outlook: Near term neutral, correction expected later

- Strategy: Sold current month 550 call for Rs 35, Bought next month 550 call for Rs 42

- Sold current month call to collect premium. Bought further month to hedge risks after expected dip later. Bear call calendar limits profits in upside breakout.

## Tata Steel Long Call Debit Spread

- Market outlook: Bullish expecting strong rally

- Strategy: Buy 1100 call for Rs 62, Sell 1200 call for Rs 45. Net outflow Rs 17.

- Bull call spread to benefit from substantial rise past short call strike. Caps maximum profit but lowers cost. Defined risk to net premium paid.

## ONGC Short Put Calendar

- Market outlook: Near term oversold, neutral longer term

- Strategy: Sold current month 120 put for Rs 6, Bought next month 120 put for Rs 10

- Put calendar to benefit from rebound after oversold decline. Longer dated put hedges risks on extended fall later after expiry.

## Dr Reddy Bear Put Diagonal

- Market outlook: Near term neutral, correction expected later

- Strategy: Sold 4400 put for Rs 75, Bought 1 month 4200 put for Rs 100

- Earned premium to fund long put. Longer dated OTM put benefits from expected decline later while short put gains if neutral initially.

## HDFC Short Put Ladder

- Market outlook: Bullish bias but unsure of upside potential

- Strategy: Sold 2400 put for Rs 50, sold 2500 put for Rs 75, bought 2600 put for Rs 100

- Put ladder to earn premium through incremental short put strikes. Uncapped profit above 2600. Secured some gains in sideways move while retaining upside exposure.

## ICICI Bank Long Put Butterfly

- Market outlook: Rangebound consolidation expected

- Strategy: Buy 940 put for Rs 62, sell 2 860 puts for Rs 35 each, buy 820 put for Rs 18

- Put butterfly construct for low net debit. Maximum profit if ICICI settles between middle short strike at expiry. Capped but defined risk on either side.

## HUL Short Call Ratio Spread

- Market outlook: Bearish view expecting significant correction

- Strategy: Sold 3 lots 2700 call at Rs 50 each, Bought 2 lots 2900 calls at Rs 25 each

- More short calls sold than long calls bought to skewnically benefit from decline. Lower net premium received while retaining downside exposure.

## JSW Steel Iron Condor

- Market outlook: Rangebound consolidation expected in near term

- Strategy: Sold 620 put for Rs 12, Bought 600 put for Rs 6. Sold 650 call for Rs 9, Bought 670 call for Rs 3.

- Iron condor constructed by selling OTM put and call. Hedged risks with further OTM long put and call. Net credit of Rs 12 earned with defined risk.

## **Maruti Suzuki Jade Lizard**

- Market outlook: Bullish bias but unsure of timing. Hedged risks sought.

- Strategy: Sold 8000 put for Rs 75, Bought 7800 call for Rs 125, Sold 8200 call for Rs 50.

- Jade lizard provided participation in eventual breakout while collecting premium via short OTM put sale. Cushioned risk on dip while retaining upside exposure.

In summary, these examples illustrate how options trading strategies can help traders benefit across diverse market conditions like directional trends, rangebound action, volatility etc. Practical application elevates conceptual knowledge to generate consistent profits.

# Chapter 6 – Algorithmic Trading

## 6.1 Introduction

Algorithmic trading refers to using computer programs and quantitative models that leverage statistical analytics to automate the execution of trade orders and positioning strategies. It is driven by data and algorithms instead of human emotions and manual monitoring.

Algo trading is widely used for short term trading in stocks, options, futures, currencies, commodities across exchanges globally. It enables identifying opportunities and executing orders faster than humanly possible to capitalize on predictable market movements. Traders can set clear rules encoded as algorithms for entries, exits and quantitatively optimized position sizing.

The key components powering algo trading systems are market data feeds, infrastructure hardware, trading software and quantitative model strategy rules. Market data feeds provide real-time streaming quotes, tick-by-tick data, historical databases and news events required as inputs for algorithms to generate trading signals.

Dedicated network connectivity and co-located infrastructure where trading servers are located proximate to exchange servers enable rapid execution and minimize latency. Robust trading software and APIs offered by brokers execute orders automatically based on model outputs.

Quantitative model strategy rules and logic form the core intelligence determining trades. Trade logic and signals are backtested rigorously against historical data to validate the strategy. Optimization techniques like machine learning can continuously improve strategy performance by tuning parameters like support/resistance levels, mean reversion thresholds, sentiment indicators etc. to adapt to evolving market dynamics.

The main types of algorithmic trading strategies are:

- Momentum - Trend following tactics capturing uptrends/downtrends across various timeframes
- Mean reversion - Statistical arbitrage strategies betting on reversion from extremes to average values
- Volume weighted average price - Achieves best execution for large orders by splitting across time periods
- Percent of volume - Slicing orders across minute/hourly volume providing camouflage
- TWAP - Averaging into position across fixed time intervals to minimize price impact
- Pairs trading - Long/short positions between historically correlated instruments
- Sentiment - Algorithmic interpretation of news events, earnings calls, analyst reports
- Mathematical model based - Complex quant formulae, predictive signals, statistical estimators

Over 2000 quant hedge funds today deploy various algo strategies. Retail traders also have access to rule-based auto trading by configuring parameters via brokerage platforms. However, prudent strategy development, rigorous back testing, evolving machine learning capabilities and risk management remains essential for long term algo trading success.

In the upcoming sections we will take a deep dive into algo trading concepts, system development, quant strategies, advantages and common pitfalls to avoid.

⊢ Ω Ω Ω Ω Ω Ω Ω Ω Ω Ω Ω Ω Ω Ω Ω Ω Ω Ω Ω Ω Ω Ω ⊣

## 6.2 Automated Trading Systems

Automated trading systems refer to technology platforms that execute buy and sell orders algorithmically without requiring manual intervention. Let's understand key aspects of building robust automated trading systems:

### <u>System Architecture</u>

A typical automated trading system consists of the following technology components:

- Pricing data feed provides real-time streaming quotes, trades, market depth required for strategy algorithms.
- Smart order routing uses logic to determine optimal route among available liquidity pools and exchanges to achieve best execution.
- Quantitative strategy module houses the proprietary logic encoded as algorithms generating trading signals.
- Order management system posts orders, manages unfilled orders and handles order routing.
- Risk management module monitors positions against risk parameters like volatility, maximum drawdowns, divergences etc. and takes automatic actions.
- Portfolio management tracks P&L, performance metrics and trading statistics.
- Post-trade analysis on execution quality,

slippage, latency and strategies.

- FIX API or proprietary broker API interfaces to place and manage orders electronically.
- Separate development, testing, staging and production environments allow building, assessing and deploying strategies reliably.

## Strategy Development

Automated trading relies on mathematical models that generate entry and exit signals programmatically. Models are developed using statistical analysis, predictive analytics, pattern recognition, machine learning and other quantitative techniques.

Strategies attempt to capture inefficiencies using market microstructure, limit order books, physical models, behavioral models, sentiment analysis etc. Strategies are coded in languages like Python, R, C++, Java.

## Back testing Framework

Back testing evaluates strategy performance on historical data. Hypothetical trades are simulated to assess metrics like profitability, risks and drawdowns.

Robust back testing incorporates accurate transaction costs, slippage modeling and avoids look ahead bias. Out-of-sample testing guards against overfitting.

## Optimization and Machine Learning

Optimization tunes strategy parameters like technical indicators, mean reversion thresholds, levels etc. to maximize returns or Sharpe ratio.

Machine learning like neural networks, reinforcement learning allow dynamic non-linear adaptation to evolving market conditions by discerning complex patterns.

Deriving alpha consistently requires continuous improvement as markets adapt. Automation makes iterative optimization viable.

## Risk Management

Automated risk management is critical to long term viability of unattended algos. Risk guidelines enforced programmatically include:

- Per trade stop loss limits based on volatility
- Maximum daily drawdown limits
- Position size thresholds
- Divergence from expected trading ranges
- Hedging of risks using derivatives
- Automatic position squaring off at day end
- Execution Setup

For best results, trading infrastructure needs to be co-located in proximity to exchange servers to minimize latency.

Sufficient processing power and memory optimizes execution speed. Multiple data feeds and brokers provide redundancy.

Connectivity management, load balancing, failover handling and alerting mechanisms prevent downtime.

## Post-Trade Analysis

Ongoing trade analysis provides feedback to improve strategies:

- Transaction cost analysis including impact of spreads, fees and slippage
- Performance attribution to identify profitable vs unprofitable signals
- Identifying flaws - overtrading, signal decay, insufficient rewards
- Assessing execution quality - delays, routing issues

By incorporating these best practices and principles while building trading systems, algos can deliver superior results.

In summary, developing profitable automated trading systems requires expertise across strategy research, predictive modeling, optimization techniques, robust infrastructure and risk management.

$$\vdash \Omega\,\Omega\,\Omega\,\Omega\,\Omega\,\Omega\,\Omega\,\Omega\,\Omega\,\Omega\,\Omega\,\Omega\,\Omega\,\Omega\,\Omega\,\Omega\,\Omega\,\Omega\,\Omega\,\Omega\,\Omega\,\Omega\,\Omega\,\Omega\,\Omega \dashv$$

## 6.3 Quantitative Trading Models

Algorithmic trading is driven by mathematical models that generate trading signals programmatically using statistical, predictive or machine learning techniques. Let's explore some prominent categories of quant models used for trading:

## Statistical Arbitrage

Stat arb aims to profit from short term market inefficiencies and pricing discrepancies between correlated instruments like stocks, futures and options. Mispricing revert back to the mean quickly.

**Strategies:**

- Pairs trading - Long/short positions taken when correlation between two historically related stocks diverges by a threshold. Eg: Coca Cola and Pepsi.
- Index arbitrage - Exploiting short term deviation between index futures, underlying basket and ETFs which realign rapidly due to arbitrage activity.
- Merger arb - When acquisition announced, target company stock converges to the acquisition price over the merger close period.

The key is identifying price divergence thresholds, position ratios and reversion time periods accurately to capture spreads when temporary mispricing corrects.

## Mean Reversion Models

These models capitalize on gap between current price and the average historical price which is expected to converge over time.

**Strategies:**

- Bollinger Bands - Revert back to 20-day moving average when price hits upper or lower bands signaling overextended move.
- Channels - Trade reversion to the mean when price hits upper or lower channel boundaries.
- Order book analytics - When limit order book is imbalanced, price reverts towards equilibrium

levels.

- Daily range extension - Enter counter trend when hourly price extends beyond daily range expecting pullback.

The degree of mean reversion, standard deviation thresholds and speed of reversion determine strategy efficacy. Calibrating to different market conditions is vital.

## Momentum Models

Momentum strategies aim to capitalize on accelerating price trends across different timeframes. Markets continue moving in same direction despite short term reversals.

## Strategies:

- Moving average crossovers - Golden cross with short term MA moving above long term MA signals uptrend.
- RSI 40-90 strategy - Go long below 40 threshold anticipating RSI to revert back above 40. Short above 90 to profit from RSI dropping under 90.
- Rate of change - Calculate price change percentage over past periods to identify growing momentum.
- Breakout strategies - Trade continuation post breakout of historical highs, channels, ranges, chart patterns etc.
- Dual long/short moving average crossovers, multi-timeframe analysis and combining mean reversion at extremes boosts success rate.

## Machine Learning Models

Machine learning algorithms dynamically identify complex data patterns, learn from past data and improve over time without explicit programming.

**Strategies:**

- ANN - Artificial neural networks with hidden layers discern nonlinear relationships like chart patterns, support/resistance levels from price history.
- Reinforcement learning - Agents learn optimal trading actions maximizing reward function through trial-and-error interactions.
- Supervised learning - Models trained on labelled price data to predict directional movement. Eg: Support vector machines, random forest.
- Unsupervised learning - Hidden relationships and price clusters identified from unlabeled data. Eg: k-means clustering.

Machine learning manages nonlinearities, dimensionality and interactions automatically. Continual learning adapts models to evolving markets.

## Sentiment Analysis Models

News analytics, social media feeds and earnings call transcripts parsed using NLP algorithms to generate sentiment driven trades automatically.

**Strategies:**

- Classify news, tweets, statements as positive/negative/neutral and trade accordingly.

- Keyword approach – Scan sources for mentions of keywords like "profit", "growth", "disruption".
- Supervised learning - Train classification models on labeled sentiment data for live inference.
- Sentiment models attempt to gain predictive trading edge over market by reacting faster to news and events. Challenges include contextual understanding, sarcasm detection and focus on material events.

In summary, quantitative models extract trading value from statistical patterns, relationships, market dynamics and alternative data leveraging the power of technology. Combining multiple factors that demonstrate persistent edge can yield robust trading strategies.

⊢ Ω Ω Ω Ω Ω Ω Ω Ω Ω Ω Ω Ω Ω Ω Ω Ω Ω Ω Ω Ω Ω Ω Ω ⊣

## 6.4 Trading Psychology and Risk Management in Algo Trading

Developing a robust trading psychology and ingraining effective risk management is vital even in algorithmic trading to grow and sustain capital over the long run.

Let's explore key aspects:

### Cultivate a stoic mindset

Algo trading detaches decisions from human emotions by following strategy rules coded in systems. But traders still need to avoid interfering with system outputs based on greed or fear.

- Accept that losses are inevitable. Focus on long term returns through multiple market cycles.
- Don't interfere with model signals based on

recent p&l. Trust the statistically valid edge.

- Avoid overtrading by letting algo run at optimal frequency and sizing rather than overcompensating during drawdowns.
- Detach ego from trading results.successful traders view systems as machines generating probabilistic profits.

## Adopt a scientific temperament

Take a research-oriented approach to algo development and performance improvement:

- Formulate clear hypotheses for strategies. Test assumptions methodically.
- Collect extensive historical data. Rigorously back test models multiple times on out of sample data before going live.
- Evaluate strategies empirically rather than relying on anecdotal experiences or cognitive biases.
- Be willing to iterate and refine strategies rapidly based on results. Automation makes large scale iterative testing feasible.

## Manage risk actively

Rigorously monitor key risk metrics and enforce prudent limits:

- Maximum capital allocation per trade to limit losses. Typically, 1-2%.
- Loss limits on open positions based on volatility. Cut losses if stop loss triggers.
- Limits on directional exposure and portfolio margin.
- Gross and net exposure management if combining multiple models.
- Per strategy position limits for diversification.
- Hedge risks judiciously by incorporating

derivatives overlays.
- Maintain trading capacity by sizing appropriately during market volatility episodes.

## Continuous improvement mindset

Markets evolve dynamically requiring models to adapt accordingly:
- Incorporate machine learning algorithms like anns which can discern new patterns and relationships from data.
- Periodically retrain models on fresh datasets to avoid model degradation.
- Analyze strategy performance attribution - which signals/rules/features are profitable vs unprofitable.
- Incorporate new data sources and strategies to diversify algos through combo model frameworks.

## Maximize implementation focus

Meticulous implementation and minimization of operational risks ensures strategies translate smoothly from theory into results:
- Invest in high performance computing infrastructure for seamless strategy execution.
- Monitor system latency at microsecond resolution. Employ smart order routing and execution logic.
- Scrutinize transaction costs like exchanges fees, brokerage commissions, spread costs and slippage impact.
- Develop robust reporting, notifications, audit mechanisms and controls for operational efficiency.
- Maintain high service levels across trading system components for uptime. Plan disaster

recovery architecture.

In summary, algorithmic trading success requires adopting a scientific, stoic and optimization-focused mindset paired with diligent risk control and operational rigor.

⊢ Ω Ω Ω Ω Ω Ω Ω Ω Ω Ω Ω Ω Ω Ω Ω Ω Ω Ω Ω Ω Ω Ω ⊣

## 6.5  Practical Guide to Developing Algorithms

Successfully developing and implementing profitable algorithmic trading systems requires expertise across multiple domains like quantitative modelling, data analysis, coding, back testing and automation. Let's go through the key steps:

### Formulating trading hypotheses

Define clear hypotheses for strategies based on economic rationale:

- Technical strategies - price takes support at 20-day moving average. Break of support indicates further downside.
- Stat arb strategies - price of security x tends to converge to price of security y based on historical correlation. Any divergence greater than z threshold presents opportunity.
- Sentiment strategies - positive news sentiments predict increase in stock price. Negative sentiments predict decline in price.

Hypotheses provide basis for coding trading rules and quantifying edge expectations like expected holding period, win rate, risk-reward ratio etc.

### Sourcing historical data

High quality data is fuel for effective backtesting.

Sources of data include:

- Brokerage apis providing tick-by-tick and minute-wise bars across stocks, futures, currencies etc.
- Exchanges like nse provide official eod datasets. Yahoo finance also offers free eod data.
- Bloomberg, refinitiv eikon, prowess databases offer fundamental, macroeconomic, earnings call data.
- Options data sources like occ. Index data from index providers like nifty, bse.
- Alternative data like prices from commodity exchanges, weather data, web scrapers.

Data needs to be normalized, cleaned and merged into a uniform backend database or data lake for strategy access.

## Coding the strategy logic

Based on hypotheses, actual trading rules and logic are coded in languages like python:

- Import historical data into pandas data frame for analysis.
- Generate trading signals based on indicators like moving average crossovers, momentum oscillators, mean reversion thresholds.
- Code entry conditions, position sizing rules, stop loss, target levels and exit logic.
- Avoid lookahead bias - use only data up to current point for generating signals.
- Modularize strategy logic into well documented functions for easier debugging and enhancement.

## **Strategy back testing**

Backtest strategy on historical data out-of-sample to simulate actual performance:

- Account for real world trading costs like exchange fees, slippage, spread costs and brokerage charges.
- Analyze daily p&l, net returns, annual returns, risk metrics like sharpe ratio, drawdowns.
- Assess return consistency across periods, win rates, loss ratios.
- Evaluate strategy behavior across market phases like trending, sideways, volatile conditions.
- Test multiple parameter combinations for optimization.

Robust backtesting provides confidence for live deployment. Post-live performance generally aligns with reliable backtest results.

## **Algorithm deployment**

For going live, trading strategy needs to be integrated with brokers and markets:

- Paper trade initially in real market environment to test connectivity.
- Integrate strategy with fix api or broker api for automated order placement and management.
- Ensure adequate infrastructure - co-located servers, redundancy, load balancing for maximizing uptime.
- Monitor logs, metrics dashboard and alerts for issues.
- Enforce pre-defined risk checks like volatility based stop loss, position limits to prevent

runaway algos.

By combining domain expertise across these aspects, systematic traders can successfully develop, backtest and deploy profitable trading algorithms.

⊦ Ω Ω Ω Ω Ω Ω Ω Ω Ω Ω Ω Ω Ω Ω Ω Ω Ω Ω Ω Ω Ω Ω ⊣

## 6.6 Technical Analysis Chart Patterns

Technical analysis involves studying historical price charts and associated statistics to identify patterns that can predict future price movements. Technical analysts believe that all relevant market information is already reflected in the stock's price based on the forces of supply and demand. By analyzing price action in the backdrop of evolving sentiment, insights can be gained into potential future trajectory.

Some of the key patterns watched closely by technical traders are:

### <u>Trend Lines</u>

**Uptrends** occur when a stock's price makes a series of higher highs and higher lows. Technical analysts draw a rising trendline connecting these ascending lows. The uptrend remains intact as long as price remains above the rising trendline support.

**Downtrends** take shape when the market makes lower lows and lower highs. Declining trendlines connect these successive lower highs. Downtrend persists as long as prices remain below the descending resistance line.

Breaking above uptrend resistance or below

downtrend support signals potential trend reversal.

## **Channels**

Channel patterns are formed when price oscillates between two parallel trend lines indicating an established trending range.

- Ascending channel with higher highs and lows identifies uptrend. Traders play bounces off lower trendline support.

- Descending channel on lower highs and lows signals downtrend. Traders sell short rallies to upper trendline resistance.

- A breakout above upper channel signals uptrend acceleration while a breakdown below lower channel indicates trend reversal.

## **Double Tops and Bottoms**

Double top forms after an uptrend when price hits a resistance level twice forming two similar peaks. It indicates bullish exhaustion warning of potential reversal. A lower low confirms trend reversal trigger.

Double bottom forms after a downtrend when price bounces off a support level twice making two similar troughs. It signals potential bullish resurgence. A higher high confirms bottom.

The subsequent breakdown or breakout from the pattern's neckline determines trading signal. Price target is projected using the pattern's height extrapolated from breakout level.

## Head and Shoulders (H&S)

The head and shoulders pattern indicates potential trend reversal marking the end of an uptrend. It is comprised of:

- Left shoulder - Initial rally forming first peak
- Head - Higher peak forming the highest high
- Right shoulder - Final peak forming lower high than head
- Neckline support level connecting troughs before and after head
- A decisive break below the neckline confirms bearish trend reversal. The chart pattern projects downside price target by measuring height of the head relative to neckline.

Inverse head and shoulders signals potential reversal of a downtrend with upside price target projected above the neckline.

## Triangles

Triangles are characterized by converging trendlines reflecting decreasing price volatility. A breakout or breakdown from triangle signals high probability continuation of preceding uptrend or downtrend.

- Symmetrical triangle forms during both uptrend and downtrend showing indecision.
- Ascending triangle marks continuation pattern during uptrend with flat upper resistance.
- Descending triangle occurs in downtrend with flat lower support signaling bearish continuation.

- Flags and Pennants

These compact patterns signal temporary consolidation before preceding uptrend or downtrend resumes. Flags are rectangular while pennants are triangular.

A pennant forms after a strong advance, indicating bulls taking a breather before renewed uptrend. The subsequent breakout above pennant resistance provides entry.

For a bull flag, the previous move's height is projected upwards from breakout to define upside price target. Stop loss placed below technical support.

## Cup and Handle

The rounding cup and handle shape signals a bullish continuation pattern with key stages:

Cup base forms as price makes a trough and consolidates in a U shape before advancing to new highs
Handle forms as price drifts sideways creating a brief pause and trigger point before eventual breakout
Entry made above handle resistance. Stop loss below low of handle. Prior swing added to breakout defines price target. Indicates bullish sentiment and renewed upside conviction.

These patterns recur frequently across charts and markets providing insightful signals about evolving supply/demand dynamics. Combining pattern analysis with indicators, moving averages and trading volume greatly enhances robustness of technical trading strategies. Mastery is built from screen time observing hundreds of examples in live markets.

Now let's examine some example chart patterns on Nifty:

- Head & Shoulders top in Nifty around 12000 level in February 2020 reversed uptrend into pandemic selloff.
- Descending triangle formed by Nifty from June to September 2019 hinted at bearishness which played out in sharp Q4 correction.
- Double bottom pattern in March 2020 near 7500 zone indicated strong support and reversal potential post-pandemic crash.
- Ascending triangle from May to July 2020 was continuation pattern reflecting bulls' resurgence culminating in uptrend breakout.
- These observations illustrate how classical chart patterns form frequently providing technical traders trade setups in all market conditions.

$$\vdash \Omega\,\Omega\,\Omega\,\Omega\,\Omega\,\Omega\,\Omega\,\Omega\,\Omega\,\Omega\,\Omega\,\Omega\,\Omega\,\Omega\,\Omega\,\Omega\,\Omega\,\Omega\,\Omega\,\Omega\,\Omega\,\Omega\,\Omega\,\Omega \dashv$$

## 6.7 Technical Indicators

Technical indicators are mathematical calculations applied to price, volume or open interest data to analyze market conditions and identify potential trading opportunities. Indicators quantify price action and momentum, measure trend strength, volatility, trading volumes and quantify supply/demand forces. Let's explore some popular technical indicators:

### **Moving Averages**

Moving averages smooth out price data by taking

average closing price over a defined lookback period. Crossovers between short and long term moving averages signal momentum changes.

- Bullish crossover occurs when shorter moving average crosses above longer moving average indicating strengthening uptrend.
- Bearish crossover happens when shorter moving average drops below longer moving average signaling potential emerging downtrend.
- Commonly used periods are 20, 50, 100 and 200 days. Price bouncing between 20 and 50 day MAs signals range bound action.

## Relative Strength Index (RSI)

RSI analyzes momentum using closing prices over 14 periods on scale of 0 to 100. RSI above 70 is overbought zone indicating potential reversal lower. RSI below 30 suggests oversold condition due for a bounce.

Divergence between RSI and price predicts trend changes. For example, price rises but RSI falls indicating bearish divergence and impending weakness.

## Moving Average Convergence Divergence (MACD)

MACD depicts relationship between 12 and 26 period exponential moving averages. MACD line crossing above signal line indicates strengthening momentum while crossover below signals building downward momentum.

## Bollinger Bands®

Bands study volatility and encompass price movement based on standard deviation of 20-day simple moving average. Price hitting upper band indicates overbought condition while lower band hit flags oversold zone. Breakouts signal continuation of trend.

## Average Directional Index (ADX)

ADX measures strength of trend on scale of 0 to 100. Values above 25 indicate building trend strength. Above 50 signals strong trend. ADX below 20 flags weak trend and choppy conditions. Trading with the trend's direction when ADX above 25 improves odds.

Now let's examine trading examples applying these indicators:

## Moving Average Crossovers

- Bullish crossover in Nifty with 20-day MA moving above 50-day MA in March 2020 highlighted trend change signaling upside momentum building.
- Bearish crossover with 20-day MA dropping below 200-day MA in January 2020 forewarned about developing downtrend ahead.

## RSI Divergence

- As Nifty made new high in February 2022, RSI formed lower high indicating waning momentum and bearish divergence. Market subsequently reversed lower validating signal.

- In July 2022, Nifty made lower low but RSI formed higher low indicating positive divergence. Bullish signal was confirmed with uptrend resumption.

## MACD Crossover

- MACD line dropping below signal line in October 2018 signaled momentum reversal and flagged bearish trend emergence ahead in Nifty, diverging from price high.
- MACD line moving above signal line in March 2020 confirmed upside momentum and bullish sentiment revival after selloff.

## Bollinger Bands

- Nifty repeatedly tagged upper Bollinger Band from October 2021 to December 2021 indicating overbought conditions and distribution. Breakdown followed.
- Sharp expansion of Bollinger Bands in March 2020 highlighted elevated volatility signaling existing trends may not sustain.

## ADX Trend Strength

- ADX moved above 25 in February 2021 indicating uptrend strength. ADX staying above 25 until October 2021 enabled riding the bull trend.
- Declining ADX below 20 in May 2022 highlighted weak trend conditions warranting caution until directionality improved.

In summary, technical indicators quantify price action, momentum and sentiment providing insights. Combining indicators with chart patterns improves robustness of trade signals. Mastery develops from screen time and observing examples across market conditions.

├ΩΩΩΩΩΩΩΩΩΩΩΩΩΩΩΩΩΩΩΩΩΩ┤

## 6.8 Technical Trading Strategies

Technical traders develop rule-based strategies using indicators, chart patterns and price action principles to identify high probability trading opportunities. Let's explore the major types of technical trading strategies:

### Breakout Trading Strategies

Breakouts occur when price closes decisively outside a critical support or resistance level with high volume. Significant continuation move is expected post breakout in direction of new trend.

**Upside breakouts** - Go long when price breaks above resistance zones like previous swing highs, trendlines, moving averages or chart patterns indicating rising momentum.

**Downside breakouts** - Look to short sell when price breaks below important supports like recent swing lows, moving average support and trendline support flagging increase in downward momentum.

Initial stop placed below breakout price for longs and above it for shorts. Book partial profits at 1:1 or 2:1 risk-reward ratio. Trail remaining position with price momentum to maximize trend gains.

## Pullback Trading Strategies

Pullbacks refer to temporary minor corrections in the midst of an established uptrend. It indicates bulls absorbing selling pressure along the way before continuing the uptrend.

- Identify stocks in strong sustained uptrend with series of higher highs and lows. Avoid choppy sideways markets.
- Buy when pullback declines to a prior breakout zone, moving average or Fibonacci retracement level which may act as support.
- Can use pullback percentage criteria like waiting for a 2-3% retracement against 20-day high to establish ideal entry in strong uptrends.
- Keep initial wider stop under recent swing low. Book profits at next technical resistance level or trailing behind price highs.

## Trend Trading Strategies

Trading in the direction of the underlying trend dramatically improves win rate. Uptrends provide multiple buying opportunities via pullbacks and dips to add to position. Downtrends offer shorting opportunities on bounces and rallies.

## Uptrend Trading

- Look for stocks making series of higher highs-higher lows indicating solid uptrend. Use ADX above 25 to confirm.
- Identify bullish entry opportunities like retest of

previous breakout acting as support or dips to rising 20 or 50-day moving average.

- Buy on pullback dips adding to position. Place initial wider stop under recent swing low.
- Book profits at potential resistance zones, previous peaks. Trail stops up but give room for trend to extend.

## **Downtrend Trading**

- Look for stocks making lower tops and lower bottoms showing strong downward momentum. Use ADX above 25 to confirm strong bearish trend.
- Enter short sells on counter-trend rallies up to the 20 or 50-day moving averages near resistance providing selling opportunity.
- Sell additional lots on continued rallies higher. Use pullback percentage criteria.
- Have wider initial stops above previous swing highs. Trailing stops down with downtrend. Cover shorts at possible support zones.

## **Momentum Trading Strategies**

Momentum traders aim to capitalize on accelerated price movements signaling strong establishing trends early on. Indicators like moving averages, MACD and RSI help time entries.

- Identify stocks demonstrating increasing bullish momentum with indicators like RSI moving above 50-60 or MACD strengthening.
- Enter on breakouts from consolidations and chart patterns. Add on pullback dips to join upside momentum.

- Employ appropriate position sizing to ride upside move. Let profits run without exiting prematurely. Manage risks smartly.

Book partial profits systematically using technical analysis principles rather than emotionally. Avoid exiting entire trade prematurely.

In summary, technical trading strategies offer diverse approaches to capitalize across market conditions combining principles of breakouts, trends, momentum, indicators and chart patterns. Mastery develops from screen time, observations and honing skill through experience.

⊢ΩΩΩΩΩΩΩΩΩΩΩΩΩΩΩΩΩΩΩΩΩΩ⊣

## 6.9 Technical Analysis Examples

Gaining mastery over technical analysis requires observing hundreds of chart examples across diverse market conditions. Here are 10 examples illustrating how technical traders would analyze and trade Nifty,

**Sensex and major stocks:**

**Nifty Double Bottom Reversal**

- Nifty formed a double bottom pattern with 2 swing lows near 7500 level during the COVID selloff in March 2020.
- The neckline resistance level to watch was 8800. A decisive break above would confirm bullish reversal.
- In May 2020, a breakout above 8800 occurred

with high trading volumes validating the pattern.
- Traders entering on neckline breakout would capture tremendous upside as Nifty hit the pattern-measured target of 10,600 in just 3 months.

## Sensex Head and Shoulders Topping Pattern

- Sensex formed a head & shoulders topping pattern from August to November 2019 signaling bullish exhaustion.
- Left shoulder peak formed in August 2019 at 39,000. The head topped out at 40,100 in September forming higher high. Right shoulder made lower high of 39,900 in November.
- Neckline support was at 38,600. Break below in December confirmed bearish pattern completion.
- Measured target based on head height projected Sensex would fall towards 36,500 zone over next few months which played out.

## Infosys Trendline Breakout

- Infosys was consolidating below resistance trendline during September-November 2020 between Rs 1100-1200.
- In December 2020, Infosys broke out above the sloping resistance line decisively with strong volumes.
- Traders going long above Rs 1200 using trendline breakout strategy would ride substantial uptrend as the breakout fueled further upside towards Rs 1500 over next few months.

## Reliance Pullback Trading

- Reliance saw a strong uptrend from April to December 2020 rising from Rs 1100 to Rs 2100.
- Within this uptrend, temporary dips offered low risk entries like the pullback to 20-day MA near Rs 1900 support in early September 2020.
- Traders buying the dip would enjoy further upside as Reliance continued its uptrend to Rs 2400 in December.

## TCS Trend Trading

- TCS demonstrated a strong downtrend from January to May 2022 making lower tops and lower bottoms showing bearishness.
- Traders could enter short sells on pullback rallies towards declining 20-day MA at Rs 3700 and ride the downtrend.
- Oversold RSI near 30 signaled potential reversal by July 2022. Traders would cover shorts near Rs 2800.

## HDFC Bank Channel Trading

- HDFC Bank price oscillated within an ascending channel on the daily chart bounded by rising support and resistance trendlines.
- Traders can buy near lower channel support and book profits on rallies near upper channel resistance.
- A breakout above channel signals upside breakout entry while breakdown below channel cues potential reversal.

## Kotak Bank Momentum Trading

- Kotak formed a bull flag continuation pattern in May 2021 signaling rising momentum ahead.
- Traders identified bullish momentum with MACD strengthening and RSI above 50.
- Entering breakout of bull flag near Rs 1850 to ride upside momentum would have yielded 5 months of gains as stock rose steadily to Rs 2150.

## ICICI Bank Swing Trading

- ICICI Bank demonstrated swing highs and lows between Rs 500 and Rs 860 range from June 2021 to June 2022 presenting opportunities.
- Traders can buy near support zone around Rs 500 for the swing up and book profits on move to upper band near Rs 860 using wide stop below recent swing low.
- The swing ranges kept repeating enabling capturing moves in both directions by selling high and buying low.

## Axis Bank Options Trading

- Axis formed symmetrical triangle consolidation indicating potential building momentum for a breakout in either direction.
- Traders utilized options to capitalize on the anticipated move by buying out of the money call and put options to benefit from a strong breakout.
- When the triangle broke out upwards in March 2021 decisively, calls paid off handsomely

capturing large upside move.

In summary, technical analysis offers a structured approach to decipher market psychology and capitalize on high probability trade setups. Learning never stops for serious technical traders as they keep observing hundreds of live chart examples to deepen knowledge.

# Chapter 7 – New Age Models

## 7.1 Sentiment Analysis Model for Trading

Sentiment analysis aims to quantify emotions, opinions and attitudes behind language using natural language processing and machine learning algorithms. In trading, sentiment models can provide an edge by analysing qualitative data like news, earnings calls, analyst reports and social media to complement quantitative models. Let's build a sample sentiment trading model:

### **Data gathering**

Relevant textual datasets required are:
- News articles and press releases related to target companies, sectors and markets from sources like yahoo finance, marketwatch, business standard etc.
- Quarterly earnings transcripts from seeking alpha, alphasense, csmar.
- Analyst reports and sentiment ratings from brokerage research portals.
- Social media posts on platforms like twitter, reddit, stocktwits about stocks.
- Sec filings like annual reports, quarterly filings also provide management commentary.

Apis like twitter api, reddit api, web scrapers help collect relevant posts and content automatically instead of manual sourcing.

### **Text processing**

Raw text needs preprocessing before sentiment analysis:
- Cleaning - remove html tags, hyperlinks, punctuation etc.
- Tokenization - break text into sentences and words using nlp libraries like nltk in python.

- Stopword removal - filter out common words like "is", "the", "at" which don't carry sentiment signal.
- Lemmatization - convert words to base form so "bought", "buy", "buying" are treated alike.
- Vectorization - convert text to numerical vectors using techniques like tf-idf before feeding to models.

## **Sentiment analysis**

Processed text is passed through nlp models to determine sentiment polarity:
- Keyword matching - count positive/negative sentiment word occurrences like "profit", "growth" or "loss", "penalty".
- Lexicon based - compare words against sentiment lexicon dictionaries like vader. Assign positive, negative sentiment scores.
- Supervised models - train classifier models like rnns, cnns on labelled sentiment data for live inference.
- Unsupervised learning - topic modelling uncovers latent topics and sentiments.
- Aspect-based - extract feature-level sentiments from text rather than document level.

The output is a sentiment score typically ranging from -1 to 1 for each data source item.
Strategy logic

Trading rules are formulated based on sentiment signal direction:
- Buy stock if aggregate sentiment score from news, social media and filings turns above neutral threshold of 0.2
- Sell if drops below -0.2 threshold.

- Consider averaging into position to account for sentiment build up over multiple consecutive days.
- Combine sentiment signal with technical indicators like rising 20-day moving average to improve confirmations.

## Back testing and optimization

- Script strategy in python and backtest on historical news data, earnings call transcripts etc.
- Optimize parameters like sentiment score thresholds, averaging window, keywords lists using grid search.
- Evaluate metrics like returns, sharpe ratio, drawdowns. Analyze strategy behavior during trending/volatile markets.

The sentiment model aims to capture market overreaction to events before price fully factors in new information. Timely identification of such opportunities provides an edge.

$$\vdash \Omega\,\Omega\,\Omega\,\Omega\,\Omega\,\Omega\,\Omega\,\Omega\,\Omega\,\Omega\,\Omega\,\Omega\,\Omega\,\Omega\,\Omega\,\Omega\,\Omega\,\Omega\,\Omega\,\Omega\,\Omega\,\Omega\,\Omega\,\Omega \dashv$$

## 7.2 Volume Symmetry Trading Model

The volume symmetry model aims to identify support and resistance zones by analysing volume patterns rather than just price action. The rationale is that volume precedes price. Let's build a sample volume symmetry strategy:

## Volume points

Volume points are prices with highest trading volumes historically. They highlight levels where maximum

activity occurred.
- Identify volume points on daily, weekly and monthly charts to gauge activity across timeframes.
- Assume volume points represent areas of interest for market participants where price reacted significantly.
- These become volume-based support and resistance zones to watch for the future.

## **Volume point reversals**

Volume point reversals occur when price approaches an existing volume point and then changes direction forming a pivot low or high.

For example:
- Price rises towards a historical volume point resistance zone but then reverses downwards unable to breach it. Signals potential topping pattern.
- Price declines towards a prior volume point support zone but then bounces back up reversing the move down. Flags potential bottoming pattern.

Volume point reversals indicate the volume zone is acting as an area of supply/demand and the trend is struggling to continue. Traders can capitalize on the reversals.

## **Volume symmetry setups**

Volume symmetry occurs when the volume profile on opposing sides of a volume point is similar.

For example, if 10 lakh shares were traded at rs 1000 on the way up and 12 lakh shares at rs 1000 on the way down. This symmetry reinforces the relevance of price level.

Volume symmetry makes volume points and reversals even more potent. Volume symmetry zones become high conviction support/resistance areas to trade from.

## Trading strategies

Trading strategies based on volume analysis:
- Long at volume point supports with stop loss below support. Book profits at next volume point resistance.
- Short at volume point resistance with stop loss above it. Cover shorts at next volume support.
- Ride volume point reversal pattern back to original support/resistance zone.
- Consider volume point breakouts as continuation signals indicating absorption of liquidity.
- Alternatively, build mean reversion strategies to capitalize on pullbacks from volume points.

Robust volume analysis examines volume across timeframes, analyses volume by trade size buckets and combines price action with volume signals using indicators like obv for high conviction setups.
The core edge is identifying one-sided supply/demand levels early where the trend is likely to reverse based on volume footprints before price reflects it.

⊢ Ω Ω Ω Ω Ω Ω Ω Ω Ω Ω Ω Ω Ω Ω Ω Ω Ω Ω Ω Ω Ω ⊣

## 7.3 News Quant Trading Model

A news quant model aims to analyze market moving

news, events and disclosures faster than the broader market by extracting signals from textual sources algorithmically. Let's build a sample news quant model:

## **Data gathering**

Relevant datasets include:
- News articles from financial portals, newspapers, websites related to markets and specific stocks.
- Earnings call transcripts, earnings releases, annual reports, quarterly filings contain useful commentary.
- Analyst reports, rating changes, target revisions from brokerage and independent research firms.
- Conference call transcripts from management speeches at industry events and investor meetings.

Web scraping, apis and data aggregators like benzinga, meltwater can automatically pull news and events from hundreds of websites into a database.

## **Text processing**

Raw text needs to be pre-processed before extracting signals:
- Remove html tags, hyperlinks and numbers using regex in python.
- Standardize variant company and person name spellings using lookups.
- Filter filler words via stop word removal to extract most relevant terms.
- Group related words under base forms using lemmatization.
- Consider weighting word importance using techniques like tf-idf.

The cleaned corpus furnishes a concise data foundation before news analytics.

## News analytics

Processed text is passed through nlp pipelines, classifiers and hand-crafted rules to detect relevant news events, statements and derive trading signals:

- Keyword based rules - scan for key phrases like "profit rise", "demand increase", "revenue guidance" etc.
- Entity extraction - identify relevant companies mentioned using named entity recognition.
- Aspect-based sentiment - gauge management sentiment on topics like demand, pricing power, margins using aspect modelling.
- Event extraction - identify events like product launches, mergers etc. Using templates and knowledge bases.
- Text summarization - extract key highlights and takeaways from long documents like earnings transcripts.

The output is concise trading signals like company name, news category, sentiment score, relevance score etc.

## Strategy logic

Simple trading rules based on news signals:

- Buy stock if relevant positive news sentiment score > 0.70 (scale of -1 to 1)
- Sell if highly negative news sentiment score < -0.70
- Consider volume and price action for additional signal confirmation.

The goal is to trade early as the market gradually

digests new information before price fully reacts.

## Back testing

- Script strategy in python and back test on historical news data. Vary holding periods.
- Optimize parameters like sentiment score thresholds, volume filters, entity weighting etc.
- Evaluate financial metrics like sharpe ratio, drawdowns, risk-adjusted returns.

The edge aims to exploit inefficiencies as market gradually processes new data that algos can trade on faster.

⊢ΩΩΩΩΩΩΩΩΩΩΩΩΩΩΩΩΩΩΩΩΩΩ⊣

## 7.4 Technical-Fundamental Blend Model

This hybrid model combines the strengths of traditional technical analysis and machine learning on fundamental data to uncover mispriced stocks.

## Data inputs

The model requires two key data feeds:

## Technical data:

- Price history - open, high, low, close prices and volumes across various intervals like 1 min, 5 min, 15 min, 60 min, daily.
- Technical indicators derived from price data like moving averages, rsi, macd, bollinger bands, atr etc.
- Chart patterns and events like gaps, breakouts, supports, resistances etc.

## Fundamental data:

- Company financials like quarterly/annual income statements, balance sheets, cash flow statements.
- Valuation ratios like p/e, p/b, p/s, ev/ebitda, dividend yield etc.
- Earnings and financial growth over historical periods.
- Macroeconomic factors like interest rates, gdp growth, inflation.
- Sector performance data.

## Feature engineering

Prepare the data for modelling:

- Clean missing and erroneous values. Handle outliers. Normalize features.
- For technical indicators, use lags like macd(t-1) as model features to avoid look ahead bias.
- For fundamentals, compute ratios from raw financial statement data.
- Perform dimensional reduction techniques like pca to avoid overfitting and reduce complexity for ml model.
- Split into train and test sets for modelling.

## Machine learning model

Train classification model to predict price movement direction. Example workflow:

- Input layer accepts financial ratios, technical indicators, price lags as features.
- Hidden layers in neural network model discern complex relationships and patterns between variables and price.
- Output layer predicts price movement direction for next day or next week.
- Use augmentations, dropout, model frameworks

like lstm, attention layers to boost accuracy.

## Strategy logic

- When model predicts upward breakout, go long at open next day. Exit on momentum exhaustion signal like bearish rsi divergence.
- If model predicts support break, short sell next day open. Cover on rsi bullish divergence.
- Limit position size and risk per trade. Sufficient backtest data required for robustness.

The blended model enhances signals by reconciling technical and fundamental viewpoints like oversold technically but strong fundamentals. This provides high conviction trading edge.

$$\vdash \Omega\,\Omega\,\Omega\,\Omega\,\Omega\,\Omega\,\Omega\,\Omega\,\Omega\,\Omega\,\Omega\,\Omega\,\Omega\,\Omega\,\Omega\,\Omega\,\Omega\,\Omega\,\Omega\,\Omega\,\Omega\,\Omega\,\Omega\,\Omega\,\Omega \dashv$$

## 7.5 Crypto-Correlation Model

This model analyzes statistical relationships between cryptocurrency and equity markets to discover leading intermarket indicators.

## Data gathering

Collect time-series price data for:
- Major cryptocurrencies like bitcoin, ethereum, xrp, solana etc. Across desired timeframes like 1 min, hourly or daily.
- Index and stock closing prices for benchmark equity indices like s&p 500, nifty 50 and select stocks.
- Macro factors like gold price, crude oil price, treasury yields, vix volatility index.

Normalizing data conventions like timezone considerations important before correlation analysis.

## Correlation analysis

Compute correlations between crypto and other assets over rolling lookback windows:

- Pearson coefficient gives linear correlation from -1 to 1.
- Spearman rank coefficient assesses monototic relationships.
- Dynamic conditional correlation accounts for time-varying relationships.
- Granger causality tests predictiveness between time series.

Visualize correlations using heat maps to identify relationships persisting across long lookbacks.

## Leading indicator discovery

Analyze lead-lag effects between correlated assets:

- Compute correlations with crypto leading other assets by different lag periods like crypto(t) vs equity(t+1).
- Significant cross-correlations with lags implies predictive potential.
- Techniques like cross-correlation function help uncover leads.

For example, if bitcoin price movements consistently precede s&p 500 movements by 3 days, it can act as a leading indicator.

## Trading strategy

Rules based on predictive relationships:

- If crypto-equity correlation is strong historically and bitcoin rising, buy equity index/stock in 2-3 days anticipating effect.
- If crypto falling, short sell equity with lagged

effect.
- Can be combined with other signals like technical analysis for robustness.

The edge aims to benefit from intermarket effects and risk asset relationships that are statistically persistent but not fully priced in yet.

$$\vdash \Omega\,\Omega\,\Omega\,\Omega\,\Omega\,\Omega\,\Omega\,\Omega\,\Omega\,\Omega\,\Omega\,\Omega\,\Omega\,\Omega\,\Omega\,\Omega\,\Omega\,\Omega\,\Omega\,\Omega\,\Omega\,\Omega\,\Omega\dashv$$

## 7.6 Insider Trading Model

This model tracks insider transactions and derivatives positions to identify informative signals for potential stock movement.

### Data collection
- Insider trade filings like form 4 from sec contain details of insider transactions in company stock like buy/sell, number of shares, price etc.
- Form 144 outlines planned sale of restricted stock by corporate insiders.
- Form 13f contains quarterly positions of institutional investors.
- Options data to track unusual options activity by insiders anticipating price movements.

Web scrapers, apis and aggregators like market chameleon track and compile insider filings data for analysis.

### Filing analysis
Extract signals from filings:
- Classify transaction as buy/sell. Filter small insignificant trades.
- Identify timing cluster patterns. For example, multiple insiders buying signals conviction.

- Assess trend in insider activity over past quarters using diffusion index.
- Analyze size of transaction relative to insider's normal transaction value and total holdings.
- Detect variability spike in insider derivatives positions indicating hedging predictive of stock moves.

The output is an insider activity score denoting bullish/bearish inclination.

## Strategy design

Rules incorporate insider signal as directional bias:
- If insider score turns significantly positive, take long position in stock anticipating potential rise.
- If insider score turns significantly negative, take short position expecting potential decline.
- Consider trading mirrors insider's actions - buy/sell same proportion as insider's transaction size.
- Use stop loss to contain risk according to market volatility. Book partial profits at technical resistances.

The edge aims to benefit from legally trading on non-public information possessed by insiders on company prospects.

## Back testing

- Collect historical form 4 filings data for strategy back testing across past market regimes.
- Optimize parameters like activity thresholds, holding periods, position size etc.
- Evaluate risk-adjusted performance and behavioral analysis of strategy.

Thorough back testing required to determine if predictive edge persists consistently after accounting for trading costs.

$$\vdash \Omega\,\Omega\,\Omega\,\Omega\,\Omega\,\Omega\,\Omega\,\Omega\,\Omega\,\Omega\,\Omega\,\Omega\,\Omega\,\Omega\,\Omega\,\Omega\,\Omega\,\Omega\,\Omega\,\Omega\,\Omega \dashv$$

## 7.7 Alternative Data Model

Alternative data refers to non-traditional data sources like satellite imagery, shipping statistics, weather patterns, online search trends, social media chatter etc. That could contain predictive signals for trading. Let's build a sample alternative data model:

### Data collection

Relevant alternative datasets:
- Satellite imagery to track activity at ports, mines, warehouses, farms, factories for volume and inventory signals.
- Gps tracking of shipping vessels, fleet activity and port traffic for supply chain insights.
- Sensor data measuring temperature, rainfall from weather stations for agricultural yield estimates.
- Web traffic and search analytics for companies, products from tools like google trends and semrush.
- Social media platforms like twitter for gauging consumer sentiment, product feedback.
- Smartphone location data and foot traffic information at retail outlets.

Many alt datasets are proprietary or expensive. Retail investors can access limited free samples to test strategies.

## Data processing

- For image data, use image processing techniques like object detection, scene classification, crops estimation etc.
- Convert unstructured data into statistical features like rainfall over last 7 days, vessel activity at port vs 4 week average etc.
- For web or social data, focus on trend statistics rather than granular value.
  Feature engineering
- Derive trading signals like % change in parking lot occupancy from image data or % increase in weather impacted crop condition reports or freight shipment volume growth over 4 weeks.
- Combine alt features with traditional signals like price momentum, moving average crossovers to improve predictability.

## Strategy design

Examples of trading rules:
- Go long corn futures if satellite data and agricultural reports predict below normal crop yield.
- Buy retail stock if google search volumes and web traffic for its flagship product rise 20% month over month indicating demand surge.
- Short coal company stock if railway cargo traffic and port volumes show declining shipments qoq signalling inventory buildup.

Robust signal selection, position sizing and risk management key to long term success.

## Back testing

- Backtest model on historical alternative data. Simulate trades, optimize parameters.
- Analyze risk-adjusted returns and compare

incremental value over just price data strategies.

The edge aims to tap predictive signals from non-traditional datasets before effects are fully reflected in stock prices.

$$\vdash \Omega\,\Omega\,\Omega\,\Omega\,\Omega\,\Omega\,\Omega\,\Omega\,\Omega\,\Omega\,\Omega\,\Omega\,\Omega\,\Omega\,\Omega\,\Omega\,\Omega\,\Omega\,\Omega\,\Omega\,\Omega\,\Omega \dashv$$

## 7.8 Twitter Sentiment Model

This model analyses sentiment and emotions expressed in stock-related posts on twitter to identify investor hype cycles and trade accordingly.

### Data collection

Gather relevant twitter data:
- Stock cashtags like $tsla or $amzn to filter posts about specific stocks.
- Keywords related to investing like stocks, bullish, bearish, long, short, calls, puts etc.
- Hashtags like #stocks, #trading, #investing, #markets for topic-specific posts.
- Usernames of influential accounts like traders, investors, analysts, media persons for expert opinions.
- Date filters to collect historical datasets for backtesting purposes.

Use twitter api or tools like twint, twitterscraper to collect filtered streams of tweet data into a database.

### Text processing

Clean and preprocess tweets before analysis:
- Remove urls, unicode characters, emojis, unrecognized tokens using regex.
- Standardize variants of cashtags like $amzn, $amazon etc. Using mapping dictionary.

- Normalize words like bulls, bullish to base form using lemmatization.
- Filter tickers based on exchange symbol reference dataset to minimize irrelevant matches.

This cleaned corpus will feed into next stage of sentiment modeling.

## **Sentiment analysis**

Apply nlp techniques to determine tweet sentiment:
- Lexicon-based model comparing words against sentiment dictionary like vader.
- Supervised classifiers like lstm neural networks trained on labelled sentiment dataset to categorize tweets.
- Assign continuous polarity scores from -1 to 1 to each tweet based on degree of bullishness or bearishness.
- Aspect-based models can provide granular insights into different features like valuation, earnings, management commentary etc.

Aggregated sentiment score time series becomes trading signal.

## **Strategy design**

Sample trading rules based on twitter sentiment signal:
- Go long stock if 7-day moving average bullish sentiment score improves above neutral threshold of 0.05 into positive zone.
- Liquidate long if bearish sentiment rises above threshold like -0.05.
- Consider sentiment acceleration and absolute thresholds based on historical distribution.

- Combine with price action signals like moving average crossovers to improve robustness.

The edge aims to ride market hype cycles as retail positioning reveals itself on social media before fully reflecting in prices.

## **Back testing**

- Script strategy in python and back test on historical filtered twitter dataset.
- Optimize parameters like sentiment score thresholds, moving average windows, stop loss etc.
- Evaluate metrics like sharpe ratio, win rate, drawdowns etc. Compare incremental value over just price data strategies.

Thorough statistical validation needed to assess if predictive edge holds consistently after accounting for trading costs.

⊢ Ω Ω Ω Ω Ω Ω Ω Ω Ω Ω Ω Ω Ω Ω Ω Ω Ω Ω Ω Ω Ω Ω ⊣

## **7.9 Technical Chart Synthesis Model**

This model uses ai generative techniques to create synthetic chart patterns which are then backtested for viability.

## **Generative adversarial networks (gans)**

Gans involve two neural networks competing against each other:

- Generator network creates synthetic data similar to original data distribution.
- Discriminator network tries to identify which data is real and which is generated.

185

The generator tries to fool the discriminator by producing increasingly realistic data. This training in adversarial settings results in highly realistic artificial data generation.

## Data preparation

Gather chart pattern data:
- Collect thousands of real chart images across varieties of patterns like triangles, head & shoulders, channels, flags etc. From historical data.
- Gather related metadata like date, asset name, pattern type, breakout direction etc.
- Perform image pre-processing like cropping pattern from full chart, normalizing size, pixel density transformations.
- Develop taxonomy and annotate image dataset for modelling.

This dataset will train the gan model.

## Chart pattern gan

Train generator and discriminator networks:
- Generator takes random input noise vector and upsamples into image dimensions using convolutional transpose layers.
- Discriminator takes real and generated images as input and classifies them using convolutional layers.
- The adversarial training minimizes generator loss for fooling discriminator and maximizes discriminator loss for correctly classifying real vs fake.

Over multiple iterations, generator network learns to

create highly realistic synthetic but artificial chart patterns with accompanying metadata.

## Strategy back testing

Now back test the model generated chart patterns:
- Perform breakout analysis on each generated pattern. Identify buy and short signals, stop loss, profit targets based on back test engine logic.
- Simulate trades and evaluate strategy performance if signals were followed.
- Assess metrics like sharpe ratio, win rate, risk-adjusted return, drawdowns etc.

This reveals the profitability edge if artificial signals are traded systematically. The generator model can be tuned further based on back test results to create higher quality patterns.

In summary, gans allow synthesis of abundant simulated chart patterns to expand strategy research and discover new technical trading edges.

⊦ Ω Ω Ω Ω Ω Ω Ω Ω Ω Ω Ω Ω Ω Ω Ω Ω Ω Ω Ω Ω Ω Ω Ω ⊣

## 7.10 Prediction Markets Model

Prediction markets are exchange traded markets where participants trade contracts on the outcome of future events. The prices represent probability estimates of the event based on collective wisdom of trades. This model aims to identify mispriced outcomes on prediction markets to trade on.

## Prediction markets data

- Collect historical price data across various contracts from prediction market platforms like polymarket, metaculus, predictit which cover topics like company earnings, product launches, geopolitical events, economic releases etc.

- Compile metadata like contract details, expiry date, settlement conditions, category etc.
- For specific companies follow contracts predicting earnings results, product announcements, m&a deals.
- When outcome occurs note the actual result to compare with prediction market forecast probabilities.

## Estimating fair value

- Analyze distribution of historical predictions for similar events to estimate a fair value range for the contract based on empirical evidence.
- For example, analysis may reveal analysts' earnings estimate beats actual result 60% of the time. So contract predicting beat may have fair odds around 40% probability.
- For one-off events like product launch, analyze analogous situations and expert opinions to gauge fair value of contract.
- Keep updating estimates as new information emerges closer to event. Maintain probability estimate confidence intervals.

## Identifying mispricings

- When prediction market contract price diverges significantly above or below the fair value range estimated empirically, it presents a trading opportunity.
- For example, if market predicts 80% chance of earnings beat but historical analysis reveals actual beat probability around 50%, the contract may be overpriced.

- Similarly, if market assigns very low probability for an unlikely but plausible event, the contract may offer attractive upside.

## Trading strategy

- Buy underpriced contracts where crowd wisdom has diverged unfavorably from empirical fair value.
- Short overpriced contracts where market odds have exceeded reasonable expectations.
- Hedge risks by taking offsetting positions in correlated markets.

The edge capitalizes on correction of collective forecast errors as actual outcome manifests. Prediction market inefficiencies offer low risk opportunities through wisdom of crowds arbitrage.

$$\vdash \Omega\,\Omega\,\Omega\,\Omega\,\Omega\,\Omega\,\Omega\,\Omega\,\Omega\,\Omega\,\Omega\,\Omega\,\Omega\,\Omega\,\Omega\,\Omega\,\Omega\,\Omega\,\Omega\,\Omega\,\Omega\,\Omega\,\Omega\,\Omega\,\Omega\dashv$$

## 7.11 Fibonacci Retracement Fractals Model

This model applies fibonacci ratio analysis across multiple timeframes to identify support and resistance levels and fractal self-similarity for trading opportunities.

## Fibonacci ratios background

Important fibonacci ratios derived from the fibonacci sequence include:

- 0.618 - golden ratio
- 0.382 - lower retracement ratio
- 0.5 - mid retracement ratio
- 0.786 - higher retracement ratio

These ratios help estimate likely pullback and retracement magnitudes in ongoing trends across asset classes.

## Fibonacci analysis

- Identify significant swing highs and swing lows on chart across higher timeframe like weekly or daily.
- Draw fibonacci retracement levels between significant swing points, projecting ratio levels like 0.382, 0.5, 0.618 etc.
- Observe how price reacts around fib levels. Levels witnessing 3 reactions indicate cluster support/resistance zone.
- Change in polarity from support-resistance at fib zone signals potential trend reversal.

Confluence across timeframe fib levels offers high conviction trade location.

## Fractal analysis

Fractals represent self-similar patterns across micro and macro scales. In trading:

- Lower timeframe like 5 min forms the micro fractal pattern.
- Higher timeframe like daily forms the macro fractal structure.
- Look for alignment and consistent ratios between the timeframe price levels and movements.
- Confluence adds confidence for both setting trade location and estimating target projections.

For example, the ratio of a daily swing leg down corresponds to 0.618 of a weekly swing projected from the same peak.

## Trading strategies

Trade setups based on multi-timeframe fibonacci

analysis:
- Enter longs at fib support zones on higher timeframe, with stop loss below micro support fractal on lower timeframe.
- Enter shorts at macro resistance level confirmed by lower timeframe resistance fractal. Define risk below micro support.
- Project upside/downside targets based on measuring macro swings and transferring ratios to micro timeframe.

The edge lies in early anticipation of turning points and price objectives using consistent human behaviour revealed across fractal timeframes.

⊢ Ω Ω Ω Ω Ω Ω Ω Ω Ω Ω Ω Ω Ω Ω Ω Ω Ω Ω Ω Ω Ω Ω Ω ⊣

## 7.12 Sentdex Trading Model

This model processes financial news and analysis videos from youtube algorithmically to generate trading signals by interpreting commentary, tone and visuals.

### Data collection

Gather relevant youtube videos:
- Channel sources like cnbc, bloomberg, et now, cnbctv18 for news and shows covering markets.
- Videos of specific analysts and influencers closely followed by trading community.
- Company earnings call webcasts, annual meetings, conference presentations.
- Filter by keywords like stock market, investing, trading, technical analysis etc.

Youtube api and scraping tools help compile historical videos data for back testing.

## Video processing

Extract useful signals from video data:
- Convert to images at 1 frame per second. Summarize key points with frame differencing to reduce data size.
- Extract audio track and convert into text via automated speech recognition like google speech api.
- Detect speaker segments like anchor, guest etc. Using speaker diarization techniques.
- Recognize broker names, stock tickers, keywords using entity recognition and supervised learning models.
- Assess tone using sentiment analysis on transcript and volume, pitch in audio track.

This outputs concise trading relevant entities, relationships and audio-visual features.

## Strategy design

Sample trading rules based on video analysis:
- Buy stock if anchor/expert mentions company positively more than 3 times in a bullish tone and shows upbeat chart patterns.
- Sell stock if speaker warns about fundamentals deterioration, regulatory risks etc. In negative tone and shows corresponding bearish chart pattern.
- Consider sentiment, repetition, emphasis of keywords along with visuals for signal robustness.

The edge aims to tap predictive signals from experts on media platforms before fully reflecting in stock prices.

## Back testing

- Build strategy trading logic in python and back test on historical videos data.
- Optimize parameters like sentiment score thresholds, repetition levels, anchor vs guest weightings etc.
- Evaluate risk-adjusted returns vs just price data strategies. Assess financial metrics like sharpe ratio, sortino ratio etc.

Significant quantitative evidence needed to validate if edge persists after accounting for trading costs like slippage, commissions etc.

$$\vdash \Omega\,\Omega\,\Omega\,\Omega\,\Omega\,\Omega\,\Omega\,\Omega\,\Omega\,\Omega\,\Omega\,\Omega\,\Omega\,\Omega\,\Omega\,\Omega\,\Omega\,\Omega\,\Omega\,\Omega\,\Omega\,\Omega\,\Omega\,\Omega \dashv$$

## 7.13 Wikipedia Earnings Model

This model scrapes upcoming earnings release dates from wikipedia to trade stocks based on the earnings surprise between actual reported eps versus consensus expected eps.

## Data collection

- Wikipedia maintains a crowdsourced earnings calendar page listing upcoming earnings announcement dates of major companies.
- Use web scraping tools to extract the quarterly earnings dates for target companies from this page.
- Supplement with historical eps consensus estimates data from bloomberg, zacks, yahoo finance etc.
- Compile actual reported eps numbers from historical earnings release statements.

This provides the key dataset for back testing

surprises.

## Earnings surprise

On each earnings announcement:
- Note actual eps reported by the company from its press release or filings.
- Compare to the average analyst consensus eps estimates for the quarter aggregated from bloomberg, zacks, yahoo etc.
- Calculate "surprise %" = (actual eps - consensus estimate) / consensus estimate

Higher positive surprise implies the company beat expectations by a wider margin which is received favorably.

## Strategy logic

Trade long stocks with favorable surprise:
- Go long stocks with >5% positive surprise the next trading day as market often reacts positively.
- The more the surprise magnitude, larger the potential reaction as expectations get massively beat.
- For negative surprises below -5%, short sell next day to benefit from potential decline as market prices in disappointment.
- Use stop loss in case surprise does not translate into actual price movement due to other factors.

The edge aims to benefit from short term price spikes as market reacts to eps surprises before fully absorbing the news.

## Results validation

- Back test strategy on past 5-10 years of earnings

data. Optimize surprise trade thresholds.

- Ensure risk-adjusted returns are statistically significant after accounting for trading costs like commissions, slippage etc.

$$\vdash \Omega\,\Omega\,\Omega\,\Omega\,\Omega\,\Omega\,\Omega\,\Omega\,\Omega\,\Omega\,\Omega\,\Omega\,\Omega\,\Omega\,\Omega\,\Omega\,\Omega\,\Omega\,\Omega\,\Omega\,\Omega \dashv$$

## 7.14 Transfer Learning Model

Transfer learning involves taking a model trained on one dataset and leveraging the learned features on a related dataset where data is scarce. In trading, models can potentially transfer insights across correlated asset classes.

### Neural network refresher

- Input layer accepts features like price indicators and technical metrics.
- Hidden layers identify patterns like support, resistance levels, chart formations.
- Output layer predicts next period returns or price levels.
- Model training tunes weights of neuron connections through backpropagation to minimize loss.
- Learned features in hidden layers retain relevance even for related datasets.

### Financial timeseries data

For model inputs collect standardized price data across asset classes:

- Equities - major stocks, sectors, indices like s&p 500.
- Commodities - gold, oil, natural gas, copper, agriculture futures.
- Forex - major currency pairs like eur/usd, gbp/usd, usd/jpy.

- Bonds - us treasury bond yields across tenors.

Feature engineer returns, momentum, volatility, technical indicators as model features.

## Model training

Train neural network model on one asset class data:
- Input technical indicators and price history features.
- Model hidden layers discern patterns like support, resistance, trend strength, seasonalities.
- Output predicts next day return.
- Save model structure and transfer learned feature representations. Do not save final dense layer weights.

## Transfer learning

Now transfer model to new asset:
- Take saved base model up till hidden layers. Do not use original output layer.
- Attach new output layer customized to new asset for return forecasting.
- Train only new output layer while freezing already tuned weights of hidden layers.

This allows hidden feature patterns learned from original asset to transfer to new asset while saving compute by avoiding full retraining.

## Trading strategy

- When transferred model predicts positive returns for next day, go long the asset.
- If negative returns predicted, short sell asset.
- Maintain appropriate stop loss based on asset volatility.

The edge aims to derive quality features from data-rich assets like equities and utilize it in trading less efficient assets like commodities where data is scarce.

⊢ Ω Ω Ω Ω Ω Ω Ω Ω Ω Ω Ω Ω Ω Ω Ω Ω Ω Ω Ω Ω Ω Ω ⊣

## 7.15 Agent-based Model

Agent-based models simulate decentralized systems composed of autonomous agents interacting based on predefined rules and evolving through competition. We can apply it to evolve trading strategies.

### Agent environment

We first design an artificial stock market environment for agents to trade in:

- Generate historical-like simulated price data across stocks using garch models calibrated on real price data to mimic volatility clustering.
- Incorporate real world features like fundamentals drifting, sudden shocks, fat tail distributions.
- Agents interact in this environment by taking trading actions based on evolving strategy rules.
- Track p&l, portfolio values as performance metrics. Introduce commissions, slippage as transaction costs.

### Agent design

Model rational profit-seeking agents with learning capabilities:

- Each agent starts with a randomized trading strategy encoded as decision rules, indicators, hyper-parameters.
- Agents execute trades based on strategy and market environment inputs.

- Strategies could range from simple moving averages to complex deep neural networks.
- Agents have memory of past performance, ability to refine strategy through experimentation and learning algorithms.

## Agent training

Evolve agent population over iterations using deep reinforcement learning techniques:
- Agents experiment with parameters and learn which actions yield highest rewards like p&l.
- Top performing strategies replicated into next generation with mutations through genetic algorithms.
- Poorly performing agents eliminated while successful ones proliferate mimicking natural selection.
- Self-play through competing agents accelerates learnings. Shared knowledge can aid ecosystem-level fitness.

After multiple generations, pooled agent strategies and knowledge converge towards highly optimized trading rules fueled by co-evolutionary forces.

## Strategy selection

Finally, analyse evolved agent strategies:
- Assess fitness based on risk-adjusted returns, drawdowns, win rate, uncertainty management.
- Select top-performing strategies for robustness tests and live trading.
- Keep strategy pool diverse for adaption to changing market dynamics.

In summary, agent-based modelling provides a simulation framework to design, iteratively improve and select optimized trading strategies leveraging ai and collective learning.

# Stock Market Fit Assessment Quiz

## Personality quiz

Approach this test with unwavering conviction and unyielding honesty. Resorting to deceit in your responses will only lead to financial loss. Embrace the truth and discover your true standing.

1. What is your primary goal for stock market participation?

   a) wealth creation in long run
   b) earn quick profits
   c) hedging existing portfolio
   d) occasional passive income

2. What is your risk tolerance?

   a) low - prefer to preserve capital
   b) moderate - willing to take some risks for growth c) high - can tolerate large risks and volatility

3. What is your primary motivation?

   a) long term wealth building
   b) earn higher than bank interest rates
   c) get rich quickly by speculating
   d) beat market benchmarks

4. Which analytical style do you prefer?

   a) fundamental analysis - analysing company financials
   b) technical analysis - analysing charts and momentum
   c) mixed - use combination based on timeframe

5. How emotionally disciplined are you?

    a) very - remain calm and stick to plan always
    b) moderately - get anxious sometimes but recover
    c) low - frequently make emotional decisions

6. What holding period do you prefer?

    a) long term investing - 1 year or longer
    b) swing trading - 1 month to 1 year
    c) day/momentum trading - within one day

7. How much time can you devote to managing investments?

    a) minimal - less than 2 hrs per week
    b) moderate - 2-5 hrs per week
    c) extensive - over 5 hrs per week

8. How frequently do you want to churn portfolio?

    a) low - buy and hold stocks for years
    b) medium - few transactions per month
    c) high - daily or weekly position changes

9. Which market capitalization companies do you prefer?

    a) large established companies
    b) mid-cap growing companies
    c) small cap emerging companies

10.     How important is liquidity to you?

    a) very - need ability to sell anytime
    b) somewhat - prefer adequate liquidity

c) not important - can hold illiquid assets

11.    Which sectors are you most comfortable with?

a)    technology, consumer brands
b)    manufacturing, industrial, infra
c) healthcare, financials
d) commodities - metals, energy, agri

12.    How diversified should your portfolio be?

a) very - across 6-8 uncorrelated sectors
b) moderately - across 3-4 sectors
c) low - concentrated in 1 or 2 high conviction bets

13.    What loss tolerance do you have?

a) up to 10% capital loss acceptable
b) up to 20% capital loss if high conviction
c) over 20% loss acceptable for big upside

14.    What is an acceptable drawdown period for you?

a) up to 3 months
b) 3-6 months
c) over 6 months

15.    What is your ideal investment timeframe?

a) under 1 year
b) 1-3 years
c) over 3 years

16.    How experienced are you with investing?

a) novice - little knowledge
b) intermediate - have basic knowledge
c) advanced - have extensive experience

17.     What is your tendency for speculative trades?

a) low - avoid highly uncertain bets
b) moderate - occasional calculated risks
c) high - regularly take speculative positions

18.     How dependent is this capital for your needs?

a) very - rely on capital for expenses
b) somewhat - have other sources of income
c) not at all - investment does not affect lifestyle

19.     Do you require regular income from your capital?

a) yes, monthly or quarterly
b) occasionally, can remain invested for long periods
c) not required

20.     How much can you commit towards investing for at least 1 year?

a) below rs 1 lakh
b) rs 1-5 lakhs
c) above rs 5 lakhs

## Scoring guide:

Add up number of responses selected:

- a options = 3 points
- b options = 2 points
- c options = 1 point

Overall score interpretation:
- 50-60 - excellent fit for stock market exposure
- 40-50 - moderate fit but develop skills first below 40 - low fit, better to explore other investment                                         avenues

# ABOUT THE AUTHOR

**Abhishek** has been a pioneering inventor and researcher in artificial intelligence for over since Inception of the Technology. Exploring the interdisciplinary frontiers of machine learning, knowledge engineering and interaction design, Abhishek was an early thought leader in trustworthy AI.

As an alpha tester for Bitcoin, Abhishek gained valuable insights into cryptocurrency and blockchain technology in the early days. He also participated as an alpha tester for many emerging AI tools and platforms.

Abhishek led multiple startups developing AI assistants and tutors, advancing innovations in natural language processing. He served as principal advisor at leading technology companies, directing confidential research initiatives focused on AI safety.

Committed to ensuring AI benefits humanity, Abhishek frequently advises policy organizations. He looks forward to democratizing access to AI through education and outreach.

Abhishek has over 2 decades of investing and trading in stock market and has been training students to make a career in stock market.

Abhishek Parihar is your trusted companion on the journey to financial empowerment. With a genuine passion for helping others achieve their financial dreams, Abhishek has dedicated himself to demystifying the world of investing and guiding individuals towards success.

Starting from humble beginnings, Abhishek's own journey in value investing has been one of learning, perseverance, and growth. Through hands-on experience and a thirst for knowledge, he has honed his skills and developed a deep understanding of the market.

Driven by a desire to share his expertise and make investing accessible to all, Abhishek has become a sought-after coach and mentor. His down-to-earth approach, combined with his wealth of knowledge, resonates with beginners and seasoned investors alike.

In "Value Investing Essentials: Principles, Strategies, and Insights," Abhishek distills years of experience into practical advice and actionable strategies. With his guidance, readers can navigate the complexities of the market with confidence and clarity.

Join Abhishek on this journey to financial freedom, where simplicity meets expertise, and empowerment reigns supreme.